T0319102

Cambridge Elements ≡

Elements in Quantitative Finance
edited by
Riccardo Rebonato
EDHEC Business School

ADVANCES IN RETIREMENT INVESTING

Lionel Martellini
EDHEC-Risk Institute

Vincent Milhau
EDHEC-Risk Institute

CAMBRIDGE
UNIVERSITY PRESS

CAMBRIDGE
UNIVERSITY PRESS

University Printing House, Cambridge CB2 8BS, United Kingdom

One Liberty Plaza, 20th Floor, New York, NY 10006, USA

477 Williamstown Road, Port Melbourne, VIC 3207, Australia

314–321, 3rd Floor, Plot 3, Splendor Forum, Jasola District Centre,
New Delhi – 110025, India

79 Anson Road, #06–04/06, Singapore 079906

Cambridge University Press is part of the University of Cambridge.

It furthers the University's mission by disseminating knowledge in the pursuit of
education, learning, and research at the highest international levels of excellence.

www.cambridge.org
Information on this title: www.cambridge.org/9781108926621
DOI: 10.1017/9781108917377

© Lionel Martellini and Vincent Milhau 2020

First published 2020

A catalogue record for this publication is available from the British Library.

ISBN 978-1-108-92662-1 Paperback
ISSN 2631-8571 (online)
ISSN 2631-8563 (print)

Advances in Retirement Investing

Elements in Quantitative Finance

DOI: 10.1017/9781108917377
First published online: August 2020

Lionel Martellini
EDHEC-Risk Institute

Vincent Milhau
EDHEC-Risk Institute

Author for correspondence: Vincent Milhau, vincent.milhau@edhec-risk.com

Abstract: To supplement replacement income provided by Social Security and employer-sponsored pension plans, individuals need to rely on their own saving and investment choices during accumulation. Once retired, they must also decide at which rate to spend their savings, with the usual dilemma between present and future consumption in mind. This Element explains how financial engineering and risk management techniques can help individuals make these complex decisions. First, it introduces "retirement bonds," or retirement bond replicating portfolios, which provide stable and predictable replacement income during the decumulation period. Second, it describes investment strategies that combine retirement bonds with an efficient performance-seeking portfolio so as to reduce uncertainty over the future amount of income while offering upside potential. Finally, strategies that employ risk insurance techniques are proposed to secure minimum levels of replacement income while allowing for the possibility of reaching higher levels of income.

Keywords: goal-based investing, retirement investing, replacement income, hedging portfolio

ISBNs: 9781108926621 (PB), 9781108917377 (OC)
ISSNs: 2631-8571 (online), 2631-8563 (print)

Contents

1 Introduction

Retirement systems are designed to provide pensions to individuals who have, in principle, stopped working because they have reached a certain age, after which it is regarded as "normal" to retire from the labor market. How to finance pensions for current retirees, how to secure benefits for workers who plan to retire in several decades and what conditions a person should fulfill to claim their pension are matters of debate with numerous economic, political and social implications. This Element focuses on a question that is often overlooked in general public discussions: how to efficiently invest retirement savings so that they produce replacement income when needed – that is, in the retirement period. This is different from the approach that begins with a quest for the "retirement number," which is the amount that an individual should accumulate in order to retire, and continues with the design of a savings and investment plan such that the pension pot can grow to that size. In this approach, the setup of the investment strategy ends up being disconnected from the income-generation objective and boils down to generic considerations on the risk and return properties of financial assets. A central idea in this Element is that there should be as much consistency as possible between the accumulation and the decumulation phases. Put differently, the investment strategy in accumulation should be organized around the objective to generate replacement income, following the principles of *goal-based investing*, which are themselves rooted in the first principles of finance theory.

So, this Element is about good investment practices for retirement. Though the subject is of general interest, it is not targeted to a general audience because it does not convey simple messages such as "product A should be preferred to a product B to be on track for retirement." In fact, the "improved" products for which it makes a case, which would better be called "investment solutions" because they take into account individuals' goals and constraints, do not exist in the catalogs of asset managers, so it is impossible to orient customers to them. The objective of this Element is to foster interest in the investment industry for the launch of new forms of retirement investment solutions that better serve the goal of generating replacement income than existing products with a retirement label.

Once genuine *solutions* to the needs of retirees and future retirees are available, the next step will be to encourage individuals to choose them as opposed to adopting default investment solutions or fashionable products without questioning their adequacy for retirement preparation. In other words, individuals should be in a position to make educated investment choices because this decision is theirs alone, just like the decision of how much to save on their own to complement state- and employer-provided pensions. But in order to play such an active role in their saving and investment decisions, individuals need at least a minimal bank of knowledge on the properties of financial assets and allocation methods. To address financial education challenges is beyond the scope of this Element, but the last section provides suggestions for what remains a task to be accomplished. The message is, after all, simple: it is well known that a balanced diet and regular physical exercise are recommended to maintain good physical condition, so it makes intuitive sense that regular contributions and investment decisions consistent with one's objectives are recommended to reach these objectives.

This Element is organized as follows. Section 2 provides a broad picture of the organization of retirement systems and reviews the demographic and economic challenges that they present, which make it increasingly important for individuals to set up savings and investment strategies to supplement their retirement income. Section 3 studies the problem of decumulation, which consists in finding a way to convert accrued savings into a stable income stream that lasts for a sufficient amount of time. It concludes with the introduction of *retirement bonds*, which play an important role in this Element and are defined as securities that provide fixed or cost-of-living-adjusted income for an individual's expected lifetime. Section 4 goes through a detailed presentation of these bonds, showing, in particular, how their price can be used to evaluate the purchasing power of savings in terms of replacement income, thus providing a series of helpful metrics to individuals who want to know if they are on track for retirement. Section 5 turns to investment strategies for the accumulation phase, which is the life cycle stage in which a person saves money for retirement, and it describes new forms of balanced funds and target date funds in which retirement bonds are used as building blocks. Section 6 introduces a more sophisticated class of investment strategies, designed to secure minimum levels of replacement income in retirement while keeping the upside potential needed to reach higher levels in favorable market scenarios. Section 7 offers concluding remarks and discusses the implications of adopting a goal-based investment approach in retirement planning. Appendices contain technical details and mathematical derivations.

2 Why Retirement Investing Matters

The merits and the drawbacks of different investment choices in the context of retirement saving are not the most popular topics in general discussions around retirement; often, these subjects are confined to debates among finance practitioners and researchers. However, investment decisions have a considerable impact on the outcome of a strategy in terms of replacement income because financial assets have very different abilities to generate stable and sufficiently large replacement income. These decisions would be irrelevant if public retirement systems and defined-benefit pension plans alone were able to support the lifestyle desired by individuals. Unfortunately, this is not the case, for a set of demographic and economic reasons that we survey in this section, and this makes it necessary for individuals to supplement their retirement income by relying on their own saving and investment decisions.

2.1 Organization of Retirement Systems

Retirement systems are organized in three pillars, each of which provides income to retired individuals. A fourth is sometimes added to include nonfinancial assets like home ownership and informal sources of income like family support. This classification is standard and was introduced by the World Bank (Holzmann and Hinz, 2005), but the Organisation for Economic Cooperation and Development (OECD) uses a different taxonomy organized around three "tiers" – the first two of which are mandatory and the third is voluntary.

2.1.1 First Pillar: Mandatory and Publicly Managed Pension Schemes

The first pillar aims to provide a universal core of pension coverage to address basic consumption needs in retirement. Social Security systems that exist in most developed countries take on this task, as part of their broader objective to reduce poverty by providing income to the elderly as well as to special needs individuals, widows, orphans and so forth. This basic pension system is mandatory, publicly managed and usually pay-as-you-go, meaning that benefits are paid by payroll taxes levied from workers and employers, plus debt if needed: thus, the first pillar is redistributive in nature. A "zero pillar" is sometimes added to the classification to encompass noncontributory schemes, which pay a minimum pension to the most economically disadvantaged elderly without a contribution condition.

Basic pension schemes generally have a defined-benefit flavor in that benefits are neither expressed as functions of the contributions made during the working period nor as functions of the performance of an underlying investment, which simply does not exist in the case of unfunded systems. Instead, they are linked in various ways to an individual's past wages and to the length of the period during which contributions have been paid. A minimum contribution period and/or a minimum age is generally required to claim pension rights, and those who do not fulfill these conditions are either not eligible or receive reduced benefits. In France, individuals must be at least 62 to be eligible and have contributed for 172 quarters to have a full-rate pension. In the United

States, credits accrue every year, depending on earnings, with a maximum of 4 credits per year, and an individual needs at least 40 credits or 10 years. In the United Kingdom, the new State Pension rules impose a minimum qualifying period of 10 years.[1] Adjustments can be applied to take into account specific situations like disabilities, unemployment periods, childcare and arduous work.

To top up the benefits received from basic schemes and improve replacement rates, some countries have set up additional pension schemes with mandatory enrollment. This was the case in the UK with the State Earnings-Related Pension Scheme until 2002 and the Additional State Pension after 2002, until they were replaced by the new State Pension in 2016. In France, the Agirc-Arrco and the RAFP (*Retraite Additionnelle de la Fonction Publique*) provide additional benefits, respectively, for private-sector workers and for civil servants. Both are examples of point-based systems, so they have a more defined-contribution nature than the aforementioned systems. In such schemes, workers earn points by making mandatory contributions, possibly supplemented by employers, and points are stored in individual accounts until they are converted into benefits equal to the number of points multiplied by the value of a single point. RAFP is a funded system, in which pensions are backed by invested assets.

2.1.2 Second Pillar: Occupational Pension Plans with Mandatory Enrollment

The second pillar consists of public or private occupational pension schemes that require mandatory enrollment from workers. The size of these plans greatly varies across countries, depending on whether employer-sponsored plans existed before Social Security (Moore, 2011). In 2016, assets in private pension plans amounted to only 9.8% of gross domestic product (GDP) in France, where this pillar is not widely developed, versus 134.9% in the US, and they reached a maximum across OECD countries of 209% in Denmark (OECD, 2017).[2]

In the US and the UK, the traditional form of private pension plans is represented by defined-benefit (DB) pension plans. In these arrangements, the calculation of benefits is based on an employee's earnings and career length. These plans are thus exposed to the risk of underfunding in case their invested assets do not generate sufficient returns for the promised benefits to be

---

[1] These rules applied at the time this Element was written (in 2019), and simplified versions of the actual rules are provided herein. Usually, not all cohorts are subject to the same rules because Social Security reforms are progressively enforced and impact more younger workers than their elders.

[2] Source: OECD, http://dx.doi.org/10.1787/888933634686.

delivered. Clearly, underfunding is ultimately a risk for pensioners,[3] so some countries have set up insurance systems to secure the payment of benefits, like the Pension Benefit Guaranty Corporation (PBGC), which was created in the US by the Employee Retirement Income Security Act of 1974, and the Pension Protection Fund, which was created in the UK by the Pensions Act 2004. Before calling on a guarantee fund, underfunding risk can be reduced in the first place by the use of appropriate asset-liability management techniques, including the construction of *liability-hedging portfolios*, which ensure that assets match liabilities. This practice is fully consistent with OECD recommendations for private pension regulation:

> The investment policy should establish clear investment objectives for the pension fund consistent with its retirement income objective and specific attributes. ... The investment objective should also be consistent with the characteristics of the liabilities of the pension fund where applicable.[4]

> A sound investment risk management process that supports the achievement of the investment objectives should be established. It should measure and seek to appropriately control portfolio risk and to manage the assets and eventual liabilities in a coherent and integrated manner.[5]

DB plans still account for large shares of invested assets in these countries, with respectively 82% and 40%, according to the 2016 figures of Willis Tower Watson (2017, p. 7). But the OECD (2016b, p. 24–27) reports that the number of participants has grown faster in DC versus DB plans since the turn of the millennium – an observation that can be repeated for all countries in which both types of plans are widespread. In the US, the number of members in occupational DB plans grew from 61,686,000 in 2000 to 72,577,000 in 2012 – hence a growth by 12% – while the number of those in occupational DC plans grew from 61,686,000 to 95,379,000 over the same period, representing an increase by almost 55%. The UK even saw a decrease in the number of members in DB plans between 2010 and 2015 – from 11,999,000 to 10,973,000 – which stands in sharp contrast to an increase from 2,360,000 to 6,931,000 in DC schemes.[6]

In DC plans, benefits depend on the contributions made by the employee (and possibly the employer) and the performance of invested assets, so that participants are more directly exposed to the consequences of poor returns. In these schemes, it is participants who bear the risk of insufficient contributions, while in DB plans, the employer has to make up for deficits.

---

[3] See the failure of the Studebaker-Packard Corporation in 2003 (Wooten, 2001).
[4] OECD (2016a), Guideline 4.6, p. 34.
[5] OECD (2016a), Guideline 4.9, p. 35.
[6] Source: OECD, http://dx.doi.org/10.1787/888933426787.

2.1.3 Third Pillar: Voluntary Saving Schemes

The third pillar includes voluntary pension arrangements that individuals set up to supplement the income they receive from mandatory sources. It encompasses a variety of financial products, not all of which are explicitly intended for retirement saving, like balanced funds and life insurance. By convention, nonfinancial assets are excluded from this list, so the World Bank framework defines a "fourth pillar" that includes home ownership and reverse mortgage.

Many of the DC pension arrangements that are progressively taking over traditional DB plans with mandatory enrollment belong to this pillar. In the US, a large number of these new DC plans are 401(k) plans, named after the section of the Internal Revenue Code of 1986 that defined them, and participation in these plans is optional, although employees are automatically enrolled and must explicitly opt out if they do not want to participate. Other examples of collective voluntary pension arrangements include the French PERCO (*Plan Épargne pour la Retraite Collectif*), created in 2006, and the Dutch collective DC (CDC) schemes. CDCs have been created as an attempt to mix the best of both worlds. In CDC plans, the employer's contributions are fixed and assets brought by members are pooled in a fund rather than being invested in individual accounts, so that the risk of poor returns is divided between contributors.

In voluntary saving schemes, individuals are responsible for deciding how much they want to contribute and how they want to invest their savings, so saving practices reflect their attitude toward personal finance decisions. As a result, retirement saving is a privileged field for studies in behavioral economics. One of the well-known features of individual behavior is procrastination, which is the tendency to postpone the decision to reduce current consumption to finance future consumption. This behavior is also present in microeconomic theories based on individual optimization, where the degree of preference for the present and the propensity to substitute consumption over time are captured through ad hoc parameters. To create incentives for individuals to save on their own, regulation usually provides some form of tax advantage to saving in dedicated vehicles. There are three main categories of tax advantages, which occur at the three stages of the life of a retirement saving plan: the first applies to contributions, the second to growth in capital and the third to withdrawals.

The advantage can present as a deduction of contributions from taxable income, up to a certain limit, like in US 401(k) plans and traditional Individual Retirement Accounts (IRAs), and in the French PERP (*Plan Épargne Retraite Populaire*) for private-sector workers and Préfon for civil servants. In this system, taxes are deferred until income is distributed in retirement, so this provision is an advantage if individuals are taxed at lower rates in retirement than during their working life, which is the case if they have less income in retirement and the tax system is progressive. Moreover, if the annual replacement income is greater than the annual contribution because the investments generated sufficient performance, the after-tax retirement income is greater than the after-tax contribution. This is an attractive feature for individuals if they roughly obey the permanent income hypothesis and elect the saving strategy that maximizes their income over the life cycle.

Tax advantage can also present upon withdrawals. In US Roth IRAs, created by the Taxpayer Relief Act of 1997, there is no advantage to contributions but distributed income is tax-free, provided withdrawals are made in a certain way that makes them *qualified*. Individual Savings Accounts (ISAs) in the UK have similar covenants, but they can be used for more general purposes than retirement saving. In France, the owner of a life insurance contract can convert it to lifetime income, but only a fraction of this income is taxed.

Finally, an advantage common to 401(k) plans, IRAs and ISAs is that dividends and interest earned and reinvested in the plans, as well as capital gains, incur no additional taxes. In France, capital income and gains in life insurance contracts are taxed when funds are withdrawn, but a tax rebate applies, depending on the contract's age.

In general, individuals can choose to utilize a variety of financial products to invest their savings. In France, the owners of life insurance contracts prize capital-guaranteed funds: the traditional ones (*fonds en euros*) are invested in sovereign bonds, but products implementing a dynamic allocation between bonds and other more risky assets like equities have emerged as a response to persistently low interest rates that do not even compensate investors for inflation. Aside from capital-guaranteed products, subscribers can save money in more risky mutual funds, invested, for instance, in equities, bonds and real estate, with no capital guarantee but higher *expected* returns.

Another extremely popular class of products is that of target date funds in the US. These funds, which are described in detail in Section 5.1, mix equities and bonds and let the equity allocation gradually decrease as they approach their target date. They have the status of a "Qualified Default Investment Alternative" via the Pension Protection Act of 2006; this means that by enrolling participants in such a fund, an employer is not responsible for losses. As a result, they are a default option in most 401(k) plans, and being a default choice, many workers stick to it.

In addition to mutual funds, which are asset management products, there exist insurance products, managed by insurers and broadly referred to as *annuities*. These are described in Section 3.2. By subscribing an annuity contract, an individual converts capital into lifetime income. In the simplest contracts, income is constant and depends on the interest rate conditions prevailing at the contract's writing date and the expected longevity of the individual, but products called *variable annuities* have blurred the line between insurance contracts and defined-contribution arrangements by linking income to the performance of an underlying fund.

2.2 Demographic and Financial Challenges

2.2.1 Demographic Context

Social Security systems hinge upon a balance between the contributions paid by workers and their employers and the benefits to retirees that they finance. But their sustainability is compromised by the general long-term trend toward population aging. The OECD estimates that in its member countries, the number of individuals aged 65 and over per 100 individuals aged between 20 and 64, a range that corresponds to working ages, rose from 19.5 in 1975 to 27.9 in 2015, and is expected to grow to 53.2 by 2050. In Japan and Korea, the ratio would even grow to 75.3% and 78.8%, respectively.[7]

An important component of this trend is the increasing life expectancy, an evolution that has been observed over the past 50 years and is expected to continue throughout the next century, as illustrated in Figure 1. By taking the difference between this value and the average effective age of labor-market exit, it is possible to estimate the average time spent in retirement – that is, the average length of the period during which an individual needs replacement income. Across OECD countries, the average retirement age in 2016 is 63.6 for women and 65.1 for men, and the two groups can expect to live, respectively,

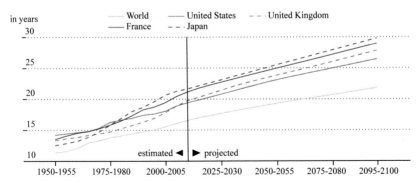

Figure 1 Estimated and projected life expectancy at age 65; data as of 2015.
Source: UNO, "Life Expectancy at Exact Age for Both Sexes,"
https://population.un.org/wpp/Download/Standard/Mortality. Figures are estimates
from 1950 through 2015, and projections are from 2016 through 2100.

---

[7] Source: OECD, http://dx.doi.org/10.1787/888933634306.

for some 22.5 and 18.0 years when they retire. The expected time in retirement peaks for France, at 27.6 years for women and 23.6 years for men.[8]

2.2.2 Underfunding Issues in DB Plans

Underfunding is a major risk for DB plans and was a motivation to pass minimum funding requirements through law. In the US, the failure of the Studebaker-Packard pension plan was even a triggering event for the passing of the ERISA, as recalled by Wooten (2001): when the corporation closed its automobile facility in South Bend, Indiana, in 1963, the pension plan did not have enough assets to pay the promised pensions, so many workers received reduced pensions or even nothing. In 1974, the ERISA expressed the first minimum funding rules, and the Pension Protection Act of 2006 introduced tighter rules, stating that DB plans must in principle be fully funded: "Except as provided in subsection (i)(1) with respect to plans in at-risk status, the funding target of a plan for a plan year is the present value of all benefits accrued or earned under the plan as of the beginning of the plan year."[9]

The ERISA also introduced new principles for the valuation of liabilities: in particular, interest rates used in the discounting of liabilities were required to be consistent with the rates of Treasury bonds, as opposed to being fixed, arbitrary values.[10] This practice gives a better sense of the size of commitments, but it creates volatility in the actuarial value of liabilities, defined as the sum of discounted cash flows, as reflected in the sponsor companies' income statements and/or balance sheets. In addition, the historically low interest rates that have prevailed since the 2008 downturn inflate this value and depress funding ratios.

Stricter funding requirements and changes in accounting standards have created a less flexible environment for DB plans, which helps explain the shift toward DC plans. In several countries, accumulated assets are insufficient to cover liabilities, and the deficit is sometimes severe. In 2016, the average funding ratio was 61.0% in Iceland, 67.5% in the US, 88.7% in the UK and 95.0% in Canada.[11]

2.2.3 Inadequate Replacement Income

Inadequacy risk is the risk of insufficient replacement income to maintain one's lifestyle in retirement. Individuals have no control over the benefits provided by Social Security systems and employer-sponsored DB plans, but as far as the third pillar is concerned, they are responsible for making saving and

---

[8] Source: OECD, http://dx.doi.org/10.1787/888933634401.
[9] Pension Protection Act of 2006, Public Law 109-280, Sec. 102, §(d)(1), p. 791.
[10] ERISA of 1974, Sec. 303, §(2)(B) and §(2)(C).
[11] Source: OECD, http://dx.doi.org/10.1787/888933634819.

investment decisions, so that inadequate income can be the result of two factors: insufficient savings and/or poor returns on investments.

As noted by the OECD (2016b), this risk is exacerbated by the fact that contributions tend to be lower in DC than in DB arrangements. Typical contribution rates are greater than 20% of wages in public or private DB schemes (e.g. 21.3% in France and 20.9% in the Netherlands in 2014, according to OECD [2015]) and are substantially lower in DC schemes (e.g. 9.5% in Australia). Inadequacy risk materializes in the pension replacement rate, defined as the ratio of benefits from mandatory public and private arrangements to labor income. This rate is generally decreasing in terms of income level, reflecting the redistributive nature of many systems, and it ranges from 42.4% to 59.9% in the US, from

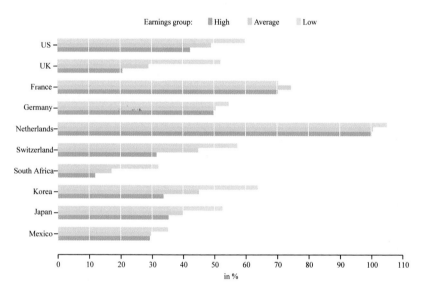

Figure 2 Net replacement rates from mandatory pension schemes, both public and private, as of 2016.

Notes: Figures are reproduced from Table 4.11 in OECD (2017) and are as of 2016.[12] The net replacement rate is the ratio of pension benefits in retirement to labor earnings for an individual earning 0.5 times the average worker earnings or less ("low earners"), between 0.5 and 1.5 times the average ("average earners") and more than 1.5 times the average ("high earners"). A detailed methodology, with assumptions on inflation, earnings growth rate, rate of return on assets in funded pension schemes, loading factor for annuities, discount rates, longevity and tax rates, is presented in pages 98–99 of the OECD report. In the US, UK, Germany, South Africa and Japan, a large fraction of the population is covered by voluntary private pension arrangements, so the total replacement rate, which aggregates mandatory and voluntary sources, is higher than the one shown in this diagram.

---

[12] **Source:** OECD, http://dx.doi.org/10.1787/888933634059.

20.7% to 52.1% in the UK and from 32.4.7% to 70.0% in Ireland (see the examples provided in Figure 2). Denmark has the highest rates, from 76.2% to 110.3%, and South Africa is among the lowest, with rates less than 35%. These numbers show that individuals are likely to experience a severe decrease in their income when retiring, unless they engage in voluntary savings plans, and as a matter of fact, replacement rates increase significantly when voluntary sources of income are taken into account in those countries where these arrangements reach a significant coverage of the population. In the US, the net replacement rate for an average-earning worker is 49.1% with mandatory sources only, but it grows to 87.1% with voluntary. But the total is still 62.2% in the UK and 65.4% in Germany,[13] and in many OECD countries, voluntary arrangements provide only limited coverage. For instance, in Italy, 9.2% of individuals aged 15 to 64 are engaged in voluntary occupational plans and 11.5% in personal plans. In France, the percentages are 24.5% and 5.7%.[14]

The focus of this Element is on designing investment strategies in accumulation, taking contributions as given. To encourage individuals to save more, for a sufficiently long period, and to choose strategies that make an efficient use of the saved money is a matter of financial education, which is not addressed here. Section 7 proposes directions for future work in this area.

3 The Decumulation Problem: How to Annuitize?

The decumulation problem can be presented as follows: starting from a capital, which is the accrued value of retirement savings at retirement time, sometimes referred to as the "pension pot", how can one generate income that lasts for the retirement period? In other words, how much can be withdrawn from the pension pot every year without the risk of outliving one's savings?

3.1 A Trade-Off between Consumption and Longevity

3.1.1 Intertemporal Consumption-Investment Planning

The decumulation problem is partly subsumed in the classical financial economics problem of planning consumption and investment over a long period. In the academic terminology, individuals attach more utility to current than to future consumption, but if they consume too much now, they are left with little to invest, so that tomorrow's wealth will be low and consumption will also be low. The intertemporal planning problem is thus to decide how to split wealth between consumption and savings in such a way as to achieve the best intertemporal utility, and how to allocate the nonconsumed part among financial assets.

[13] Source: OECD, http://dx.doi.org/10.1787/888933634059.
[14] Source: OECD, http://dx.doi.org/10.1787/888933634629.

It is interesting to note that consumption and investment decisions are intertwined: at each date, the agent must not only decide how much to consume versus how much to save, but also how to invest savings. Thus, the decision of how to invest savings – the "portfolio optimization problem" – is treated as equally important as the decision of how much money to put aside, although casual observation suggests that individuals regard it as a second-order problem and focus on how much they should save.

Optimizing intertemporal consumption and investment requires a significant mathematical effort to model individual preferences through a utility function, to specify how utilities from consumption at different dates aggregate into a single metric that can be optimized, to model uncertainty in the future returns of financial assets, and eventually to solve a utility maximization problem in which the control variables are the consumption process and the portfolio composition. In the simplest case, welfare is a weighted sum of all expected utilities from consumption levels at all future dates, with nearer dates contributing more than remote dates. The optimization program to solve can be written as

$$\max_{\substack{c_0,\ldots,c_{\tau-1} \\ w_0,\ldots,w_{\tau-1}}} \mathbb{E}\left[\sum_{t=0}^{\tau-1} e^{-\beta t} u(c_t)\right], \quad \text{subject to } W_{t+1} = [W_t - c_t] \times [1 + r_{p,t+1}],$$

(3.1)

where $\mathbb{E}$ denotes the expectation operator, τ is the horizon, c_t is consumption at date t, w_t is the portfolio composition at date t, W_t is before-consumption wealth in date t, β is a positive coefficient that reflects the preference for current consumption and $r_{p,t+1}$ is the return on the financial portfolio between dates t and $t + 1$, which depends on the portfolio composition.

An attractive feature of the approach is that it can accommodate many variations in preferences. Program (3.1) assumes no utility from terminal wealth (the bequest), so the optimal consumption and investment plan will imply that final wealth is exactly zero. If the agent derives some utility from terminal wealth (e.g. because he/she wants to leave some legacy to heirs), the objective function can be modified by introducing an additional term $\mathbb{E}[u(W_\tau)]$. It is also possible to specify a different form for the function that aggregates utilities over time, instead of assuming that they simply add up. One can also introduce habit formation, to limit fluctuations in consumption over time, and a subsistence level to avoid low consumption levels in bad times. But these features are added at the cost of increasing technical complexity, and even in the simplest case of time-additive preferences and an economy with constant investment opportunities, the solution to the expected utility maximization problem requires advanced mathematical tools like optimal stochastic control. Seminal contributions are due to Samuelson (1969), Merton (1969) and Merton (1973), and numerous subsequent papers have refined the modeling assumptions and solution techniques.

The optimality conditions imply that at each point in time, the marginal utility of consumption must equal the marginal utility of savings – for the investor could reallocate wealth between consumption and savings to achieve higher welfare if one of the two marginal utilities were greater. But marginal utility is always a decreasing function, as a result of gradual satiation: agents derive less additional welfare from having more to eat after a good meal than when they are hungry. So, optimal consumption is a decreasing function of the marginal utility of savings, and since marginal utility of wealth is itself a function of wealth (it is decreasing too), optimal consumption ends up being a function of wealth. This conveys an important message: consumption must adjust to wealth at each point in time, and it is increasing in wealth. To find the exact form of the function that maps wealth into consumption, one has to go solve the model equations.[15] This conclusion makes intuitive sense, but it is at odds with much of conventional financial advice on decumulation, which seeks to calculate a fixed, or inflation-adjusted, amount that can be withdrawn every year from a portfolio without running a deficit (see Section 3.3).

3.1.2 Uncertain Horizon

An additional difficulty arises in the decumulation problem, owing to the uncertain horizon: uncertainty over death time adds to the uncertainty over the returns that savings can generate in the future, so that it is even more difficult for individuals to make a decision on how much to withdraw every year. For instance, if a just-retired individual has $200,000 of savings and expects to live for some 20 years – the average life expectancy at 65 in the United States – he or she can withdraw $10,000 per year, assuming a zero rate of return on savings to simplify. But if he/she is unfortunate enough to pass away after 10 years only, he/she will have missed an opportunity to withdraw another $10,000 per year and to improve his/her lifestyle. Conversely, if he/she lives until 90, he/she will run out of money after the first 20 years and will know after the fact that the appropriate withdrawal rate was $8,000 per year. The case of an uncertain horizon has been considered in the theoretical literature on intertemporal

---

[15] See Equation (48), p. 390, of Merton (1973) for an explicit relation between consumption and wealth in the special case of "hyperbolic risk aversion" preferences.

optimization (see e.g. Blanchet-Scalliet et al. 2008), and it brings in new mathematical technicalities because one has to model uncertainty in the horizon and to specify how it interacts with other sources of randomness.

3.1.3 Limits to Applicability

While these models provide a solution to the dilemma between consumption and saving grounded in clean economic principles, this theoretical answer cannot be used to solve the decumulation problem in practice. Indeed, the optimal consumption rate is not robust to errors in assumptions. For instance, if an individual wrongly assumes that expected returns and volatilities of financial assets are constant, he/she will consume capital at the rate returned by the model of Merton (1969), but this rate will be too small or too large with respect to the rate consistent with the actual dynamics of the economy. Thus, he/she is back to the risk of outliving his/her expenses. Moreover, the optimal withdrawal rate can greatly vary from one period to the other because it depends on the wealth level and the state of the economy in this period, but most individuals prefer to plan their budget by having steady income in mind and have limited tolerance for adjustment of their consumption in tough times.

3.2 Traditional Annuities

An annuity is an insurance contract by which an individual pays a premium to a life insurance company in exchange for payments to be received for a period specified in the contract. There are various types of contracts, which differ through the schedule of premia; the shape of the benefits, which can be fixed or variable; and the period over which they are paid. Life annuities solve the problem of early resource depletion in the presence of longevity risk, by guaranteeing income for the annuitant's lifetime. They can be *immediate* if payments start immediately after the premium is paid, or *deferred* if a period, which can range from a few to more than thirty years, takes place between the premium and the first payment. Some deferred annuities allow the premium to be split in several money deposits. Deferred annuities are intended for two populations. First, they are of interest to individuals who are still in the accumulation or the transition period, say from 45 to 60 years, and wish to secure income starting when they retire, around age 65. Second, they can be used by individuals in the transition or the decumulation phase who want to lock income starting later in the retirement period, say at age 75, 80 or 85, when they anticipate an increase in their income needs to finance health care or nursing.

The big selling point of life annuities is that they provide fixed income for an individual's lifetime, and that the annuitant knows on the purchase date how much he/she will get per dollar given to the insurer. A cost-of-living adjustment can be introduced in the form of a fixed growth rate in payments (e.g. 2% or 3% per year), so as to provision for expected inflation and protect the purchasing power of benefits. Thus, annuities free the investor from the task of converting capital into regular income, which is a non-trivial problem to solve, as Section 3.3 explains, and they avoid the risk that an individual can outlive his/her assets. It is the insurer who manages the longevity risk by pooling individuals together, so that premia from clients who die early can be used to pay benefits to those who live longer than expected. Thanks to risk pooling, an individual has access to a higher payout than with self-insurance.

3.2.1 Annuity Pricing

Because of risk pooling, the actuarial valuation of an annuity is based on the assumption that a person will live for their full life expectancy. Mathematically, if M_i is the benefit paid in i periods from now, r_i is the continuously compounded interest rate with i-period maturity and p_i is the probability for an individual to be still alive in i periods, then the actuarial price of an immediate annuity starting to pay in period 1 is

$$\sum_{i=1}^{n_{\max}} M_i \, e^{-i r_i} p_i,$$

where $n_{\max}$ is the maximum number of periods that an individual is assumed to live, implied for instance by a maximum age of 120.

The pricing of annuities depends on the discount rates, which can be Government or corporate rates, and the mortality table, which depends on the population considered.[16] To anticipate adverse selection problems that arise because annuity buyers tend to be healthier and wealthier than the rest of the population, a general mortality table is not appropriate here and has to be replaced by an annuitant mortality table. Calculation of survival probabilities from death rates per age group can also involve subtleties because death rates are expected to decrease in the future with respect to the current experience, as a result of medical progress and (hopefully) a healthier lifestyle.[17]

---

[16] For the United States, a large sample of mortality tables can be found on the Society of Actuaries website, at https://mort.soa.org/.

[17] For instance, a possible choice to price annuities in the United States would be the 2012 Individual Annuitant Mortality Table and the Scale MP 2014 projected reduction factor in mortality rates.

3.2.2 The Annuity Puzzle

In practice, and despite their obvious advantage to secure income, annuities are not a popular insurance product. This low demand can be explained by a combination of factors. First, it can be difficult for annuitants to figure out whether the price is fair, given the amount of assumptions involved in the pricing, regarding in particular mortality, and the presence of various fees. Second, if an individual dies early, he/she will receive benefits for a short time, while most of the invested capital remains the insurer's property. This explains why annuity buyers tend to be in better health and expect to live longer than the general population, thereby ruling out those in worse physical condition, who would be the "good" risks from the insurer's perspective. Third, income is guaranteed only to the extent that the insurer is solvent, and it is reasonable to think that differences in ratings across companies account for some fraction of the differences in their annuity quotes, with low-rated companies needing to promise higher benefits for the same premium. Last, annuities are rigid products, by which the income level is locked in advance, so that the buyer cannot take advantage of other investment opportunities, like the equity market. It is still possible to terminate the contract early, but this incurs substantial surrender charges: the period in which these charges apply can be as long as 7 to 10 years, and the charge is a percentage of the invested capital, which decreases by 1% every year and ends at zero. Thus, it begins at 7% for a 7-year surrender period.

All these factors lead to low participation in the annuity market. Using the 2006 Health and Retirement Study HRS/AHEAD survey, Pashchenko (2013) reports that 7.8% of US individuals aged 70 and older report that they receive income from annuities. Interestingly, participation increases with income, but even if the top 20% income group, it is still 15.9%. Making annuity purchases compulsory forces individuals to get past their reluctance but raises other problems. When forced annuitization was abolished in April 2014 in the UK, the Financial Conduct Authority pointed that competition between providers was limited and that about 60% of individuals did not take advantage of the opportunity to shop around, ending up with poor returns on their investments.

3.2.3 Annuities with Guarantees, Variable Annuities

Alternative forms of annuities mitigate the aforementioned concerns. In survivor annuities, both spouses are insured, and part of benefits are passed along to the surviving spouse in case one of the annuitants dies. Annuities with a guaranteed period (e.g. of 10 or 20 years) guarantee that if the annuitant dies within this period, benefits will be paid to heirs for the rest of the period. Of course, these guarantees imply a reduction in benefits with respect to the case where payments stop upon the annuitant's death.

Another class of contracts, called *variable annuities*, enable annuitants to take advantage of the performance of financial markets, in particular equity and bond markets: during the accumulation phase, a variety of investment options are available for the premia, and at the beginning of the payout phase, the annuitant may choose to receive benefits in the form of a lump-sum payment or in the form of periodic income, either fixed or indexed on the performance of the underlying investment supports. These contracts also benefit from a tax deferral regime, meaning that taxes on income and capital gains from investment are deferred until funds are withdrawn, whether as a lump sum or as a stream of payments. This feature allows to accumulate capital at a higher rate, and Appendix A.1 shows that if funds are withdrawn at the beginning of the payout phase and taxes are applied at this time, the after-tax wealth left to the investor is greater than if gains had been taxed every period. However, variable annuities are complex products that carry more fees than plain annuities, in addition to the fees charged by the underlying mutual funds, which reduces their appeal.

3.3 Heuristic Spending Rules

If individuals do not purchase an annuity from a life insurer, they are left with the problem of self-annuitizing their savings in such a way that they do not run out of money. This section reviews several spending rules with their shortcomings.

3.3.1 Spend Interest Only

An obvious way to eliminate the concern over longevity risk is to spend only income from investments, like stock dividends and bond coupons, and to refrain from depleting the invested capital. One can also allow for spending capital gains instead of reinvesting them, in which case the value of savings stays flat. When the investment vehicle is a mutual fund that does not distribute dividends and coupons and automatically reinvests them, it is equivalent to just spend the capital gain – which is a total return here – and to spend the dividends and coupons paid by the fund's constituents, plus any capital gains.

This approach has the twofold advantage that capital can last forever and that the individual can pass it to his/her heirs. On the downside, a strict application of this rule means that nothing can be withdrawn in years where no income is paid and returns are negative, and more generally, the annual withdrawal can fluctuate considerably if the returns of the underlying investment are volatile. The second limitation is that the total return on a portfolio, which is the sum of price return and the income rate, is usually a few percentage points, so it takes a large amount of invested money to earn a decent income.

As their name indicates, fixed-income securities like Government bonds of high-rated countries provide steady income in the form of typically semian-nual or annual coupons, with limited risk of default, but in a low interest-rate environment, coupon rates are low, so a large capital must be invested to meet spending goals. For instance, if the individual estimates than he/she needs to withdraw $30,000 per year and invests in a bond that pays an annual coupon of 3%, he/she must purchase bonds for a total face value of

$$\frac{30,000}{0.03} = \$1,000,000.$$

If the bond sells close to par, the cost for the investor is about $1,000,000. But few individuals can have a million dollars accumulated by the time they retire, so the strategy of spending interests only is too expensive for them. Most individuals cannot afford relying only on interests and need to deplete capital to sustain their spending target. In fact, bonds eventually repay principal at maturity, but this creates a large cash flow, much bigger than what the investor actually needs at this time, which occurs after a series of smaller cash flows. This observation is one of the main reasons for the introduction of *retirement bonds* in Section 3.4.

In addition to the problem of unequal cash flows, fixed-income bonds have two other shortcomings in the context of retirement saving. First, nominal bonds, which are by far the most widespread form of Government bonds, pay constant coupons, but over decumulation periods that span two decades or more, inflation is not negligible and erodes the purchasing power of income. Inflation-indexed bonds exist, but they are not as widely developed, and they can come with negative real rates, meaning that protection against inflation risk is costly for the investor. Second, regular bonds have a fixed term, so they do not address the longevity problem.

3.3.2 Assume a Fixed Rate of Return

Many online retirement calculators allow individuals to estimate their replace-ment income from their amount of retirement savings, the duration of the decumulation period and the rate of return on their financial portfolio during decumulation. A conservative assumption is that savings produce no interest at all in retirement. If the decumulation period is τ years long and wealth at the start is W_0, the annual withdrawal that exhausts savings in τ years is sim-ply wealth divided by the length of the period, W_0/τ. For instance, if W_0 is

$200,000 and τ is 20 years, the individual can withdraw $10,000 every year and will end up with zero wealth.

But the assumption of a zero rate of return throughout the decumulation phase seems too conservative, since even a money market account earns some interest rate. A more general assumption is that the portfolio earns an annual return r, taken to be its annual expected return. Appendix A.2 derives the expression for the maximum annual withdrawal as a function of the number of years, τ, the pre-retirement wealth, W_0, and the assumed rate of return, r:

$$c = W_0 \frac{1 - [1 + r]^{-1}}{1 - [1 + r]^{-\tau}}. \tag{3.2}$$

Figure 3 shows how the withdrawal rate, defined as c/W_0, depends on the rate of return. Assuming a positive value mechanically raises the maximum withdrawal with respect to the situation where a zero return is assumed, but the output strongly depends on the assumed value.

This dependence is an important limitation in the analysis because overestimating the rate of return leads to early depletion of the pension pot. Consider, for instance, an investor endowed with $300,000 at the start of decumulation, who assumes a 7% rate of return, while the actual rate is 6%. He/she withdraws $300,000 \times 8.225\% = \$24,675$ every year. By Equation (A.2) in the Appendix, savings after t years are

$$W_t = [1 + r]^t W_0 - c \frac{[1 + r]^t - 1}{1 - [1 + r]^{-1}},$$

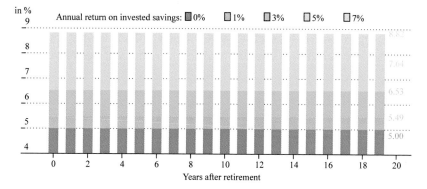

Figure 3 Withdrawal rate that exhausts savings in 20 years as a function of the annual rate of return on savings.

Notes: The withdrawal rate is the percentage of the value of savings at the start of decumulation that can be withdrawn every year for 20 years. It is calculated under five assumptions for the annual rate of return on savings.

where W_0 is \$300,000, r is 6% and c is \$24,675. By trial and error, it is found that W_{17} is positive, while W_{18} is negative. So, the wrong assumption implies that the withdrawal rate can only be sustained for 17 years, that the investor has to cut spending in year 18 and that he/she lacks resources for years 19 and 20. The situation is even more dramatic if the actual rate of return turns out to be 5% instead of 7%, since savings are depleted after 15 years only. Given that expected returns are generally very imprecisely estimated, an error margin of 2 percentage points is realistic.

3.3.3 Search for a Sustainable Withdrawal Rate

Rather than coping with the difficult problem of forecasting the return on his/her portfolios during the decumulation period, an investor may look at historical data and try to estimate a withdrawal rate that is sustainable for a given period of time. This approach has largely been used in the literature on spending rules, and it has led to the "4% rule", which is popular among financial advisors and is described in the next section.

Appendix A.2 shows that if the portfolio is invested in a fund whose annual return in year t is r_t, the maximum amount that can be withdrawn every year for τ years is

$$c = \frac{W_0}{1 + \sum_{t=1}^{\tau-1} \prod_{s=1}^{t} [1 + r_s]^{-1}}. \qquad (3.3)$$

When the annual return is constant and equal to r, we are back to the expression given in Equation (3.2), and if it is zero, the annual withdrawal is W_0/τ.

The problem with the annual spending in Equation (3.3) is that it is known ex post, while the investor must decide at the start of decumulation how much to consume every year. So, the approach is to look at the fund's historical performance in order to find a lower bound for the right-hand side of Equation (3.3) and infer a withdrawal rate that can be sustained for τ years. This is done in Figure 4, for three asset classes: cash, US Treasuries and US equities. US data is used so as to work with long time series. Each point of the horizontal axis represents a retirement date, and the decumulation period spans the 20 years after this date. For each decumulation period, the right-hand side of Equation (3.3) is calculated. This value is only known in hindsight, at the end of the decumulation period, so it cannot be taken as the withdrawal rate that a cash, bond or equity investor would set up at retirement for the next 20 years. The point conveyed by this graph is that withdrawal rates largely depend on the period considered, so that the rate calculated from past data cannot be taken as a good proxy for the rate that applies over the coming

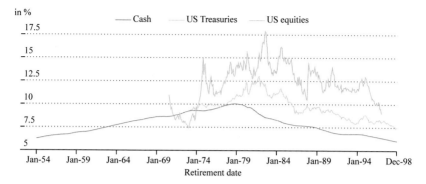

Figure 4 Withdrawal rate that exhausts savings in 20 years starting at the retirement date, per investment support, from January 1954 to December 1998.

Source: The withdrawal rate is the percentage of the value of savings at the retirement date that can be withdrawn every year for 20 years while preserving nonnegative savings. It is discovered only at the end of the decumulation period, 20 years after the retirement date on the horizontal axis, because the returns on the various investments are only known ex post. Cash is a daily rollover of 3-month Treasury bills, US Treasuries are represented by the Barclays US Treasury index with coupons reinvested and US equities are represented by a cap-weighted index of the 500 US largest stocks, with dividends reinvested. The equity index is retrieved from the long-term track records of the ERI Scientific Beta database.

period, whether it is too high, leading the individual to early shortfall, or too low, leading to unduly prudent spending of resources. The latter situation is arguably less problematic than a shortfall since a surplus can always be used for the period of life that comes after the first 20 years of retirement, or passed to heirs, but it is still unsatisfactory because the individual misses an opportunity to enjoy a better lifestyle. Time variation in withdrawal rates is yet another illustration of the saying that "the past does not reliably predict the future."

For cash, withdrawal rates have been decreasing since 1980, a trend that follows the decrease in interest rates, and this can lead to overoptimistic forecasts of withdrawal rates. For instance, an investor retiring in 1996 and asking how much he/she could withdraw every year from 1996 through 2016 could look at the rate that was sustainable in the period from 1976 to 1996. This value is shown at the January 1976 point in the plot, at 9.92%. But the data show that the maximum rate that can be sustained between 1996 and 2016 is 7.96%, the value read in January 1996. With these dates, bond and equity investors face a similar problem. Looking at the data from 1976 to 1996, they would conclude that they can withdraw respectively 9.46% and 12.12% of their initial savings amount from their pension pot every year from 1996 to 2016, but in hindsight, the maximum rates for the period from 1996 to 2016 turned out to be 6.54% and 10.47%. By withdrawing 9.46% and 12.12%, the investors would not be able to sustain a constant spending amount for 20 years and would fall short of resources before the term.

3.3.4 The 4% Rule

The 4% rule is an example of a spending rule based on the examination of past returns, but it is so popular that it deserves separate description. Credit is given to Bengen (1994) for introducing this advice for individuals targeting a 30-year decumulation period and investing from 50% to 75% of their savings in equities, with the rest in intermediate-term Treasury notes. Bender goes on to say that "a first-year withdrawal of 4 percent, followed by inflation-adjusted withdrawals in subsequent years, should be safe." In support for this claim, he reports that this spending rate has never exhausted assets in less than 30 years in historical samples. A 3% spending rate is too conservative because it lets assets last for some 50 years, which is well beyond life expectancy at retirement, and rates greater than 4% lead to shortage before 30 years in some samples. These values are estimated by running experiments similar to those of Figure 4, by adjusting assumptions: the investment vehicle is a balanced stock-bond fund, as opposed to being pure cash, equities or bonds; the decumulation period is 30 years instead of 20; and withdrawals after the first year are adjusted for inflation.

This and other related rules pose two problems. First, even if they are historically successful, they have a non-zero probability of leaving the individual with a deficit before the end of decumulation, since one cannot completely eliminate the possibility of bear markets, even more severe than those that occurred in the past. In the presence of such extreme events, an individual would be unable to sustain the specified spending rate for the whole decumulation period. Tautologically, this situation never occurs in historical data if the spending rate is appropriately selected, but Monte-Carlo simulations can reveal scenarios in which the heuristic rule fails.

This problem can be mitigated by using a conservative estimate for the spending rate, typically by rounding it to the nearest smaller integer – hence the 4%. But we then come across the second issue, which is that a conservative estimate will lead to surpluses in some states of the world, which is admittedly less a problem than a deficit but still signals an inefficient use of resources in these scenarios. As Scott, Sharpe and Watson (2009) explain, the cost of this inefficiency can be estimated by taking the present value of the surplus. By absence of arbitrage opportunities, it holds that

Initial savings = Present value of spending + Present value of surpluses,

so if the second term in the right-hand side is positive, it can be reallocated to the first one so as to increase the annual spending and make a better use of savings. The substitution of a higher withdrawal rate for surpluses results in improved welfare for the investor if welfare is increasing more in terms of the annual consumption level than in the final bequest. This is generally the case, as the literature on decumulation considers the achievement of consumption objectives to be a more important goal than bequest.

The core issue is put as follows by Scott, Sharpe and Watson (2009, p. 32): "Supporting a constant spending plan using a volatile investment policy is fundamentally flawed." So, the problem is not so much whether the recommended spending rate should be estimated from historical data or from Monte-Carlo simulations, or whether it should be a round or a decimal number. The problem is that for typical portfolios invested in stocks and/or bonds, any fixed rate will result in deficits in some scenarios and in surpluses in others. With such portfolios, spending should in fact adjust to current wealth, as it does in the Merton's model (see Section 3.1), so that final wealth after all withdrawals is exactly zero in all states of the world. If individuals target a *fixed* consumption level, in nominal or in real terms, they should first seek an investment strategy in decumulation that effectively allows constant withdrawals to be made.

3.4 Retirement Bonds: A New Asset to Secure Replacement Income

3.4.1 When Insurance against Longevity Risk Is Not Needed

In the presence of longevity risk, the annuitization problem is solved by purchasing a life annuity. In particular, deferred annuities allow investors to secure lifetime income that starts in the future, when they expect they need it. But a case can be made that an insurance contract is not needed to secure steady income for a fixed period of time (e.g. for a period that coincides with life expectancy in the population at retirement age). Consider an individual aged 55 in 2019 and planning to retire at age 65, thus in 2029. He/she needs retirement income starting in 2029 and anticipates that his/her life expectancy at that age will be about 20 years based on 2019 figures, or closer to 21 years based on projections for 2029 (see Figure 1). Depending on the value retained, this implies a decumulation period that extends until 2048 or 2049. To generate fixed income for a predefined period such as 2029–48 or 2029–49, the individual does not need any insurance against longevity risk.

The risk for anyone wanting to secure income starting in the future is the risk of changing interest rates. Indeed, it is the term structure of default-free interest rates at a given point in time, identified with the term structure of Government bond rates, that determines the periodic income that an investor can receive per dollar of capital invested at this time. But a not-yet-retired individual does not know what interest rates will be when he/she retires, so he/she does not know how much income each dollar of savings can purchase, let alone the number of dollars of savings he/she has accumulated by then. In fact, the biggest risk is the risk of decreasing rates, because lower rates imply less income. So, an individual still in the process of accumulating funds and targeting fixed income for a fixed period only needs protection against interest rate risk. Specifically, he/she needs a hedge against nominal rate risk if he/she targets income cash flows fixed in nominal terms, which includes the case where cash flows grow at a fixed annual rate, and he/she needs a hedge against real rate risk if he/she targets cash flows indexed on realized inflation. These risks are purely financial, so they do not require a contract from an insurance company.

3.4.2 Retirement Bond Cash Flows

Figure 5 shows how the cash flows of a lifetime annuity can be split in two series: the first series spans the first twenty years of retirement and the second one corresponds to "late life," here defined as the lifetime beyond life expectancy, and consists of an uncertain number of years. In this example, a cost-of-living adjustment is applied as an annual 2% growth rate in

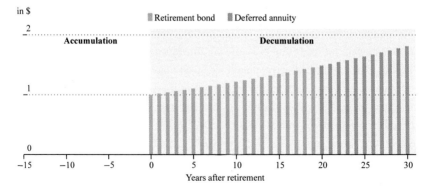

Figure 5 Cash flows of a retirement bond and a deferred annuity.
Notes: Replacement income is normalized to $1 per year and includes an adjustment for the cost of living of 2% per year. For the purpose of illustration, the total retirement period (highlighted in gray) is assumed to be thirty years, but it is actually uncertain, due to longevity risk.

the nominal value of cash flows, so as to provision for long-term expected inflation. The *retirement bond* is defined as a security that delivers the first twenty cash flows. A series of recent articles has introduced these bonds under names such as "Bonds for Financial Security" (Muralidhar, 2015; Muralidhar, Ohashi and Shin, 2016), "Standard of Living indexed, Forward-Starting, Income Only Securities" (Merton and Muralidhar, 2017), or a merge of the two, "BFFS/SeLFIES" (Kobor and Muralidhar, 2018).

3.4.3 Retirement Bonds versus Deferred Annuities

A common characteristic of a retirement bond and a deferred annuity is that they both generate income starting in the future, when the individual retires. A major difference is that the retirement bond produces income for a fixed period, as opposed to for the individual's lifetime. By foregoing protection against longevity risk, retirement bonds avoid a major source of the complexity in annuity pricing, namely the mortality assumptions, and are thus easier to understand for individual investors and to price by providers. For this reason, they are subject neither to the fees charged by insurance companies for the specific complexity involved in pricing contracts based on a mortality table, nor to those charged to provision for unexpected longevity.

Other differences exist between the retirement bond and an annuity, which should make the former more attractive to individuals if they were available in financial markets and, in particular, if they were issued by Governments. These arguments are exposed in detail by Muralidhar, Ohashi and Shin (2016). First, if they are issued in sufficiently large amount at a sufficiently high frequency with a variety of retirement dates, they will be liquid and fungible securities with publicly available prices. This stands in contrast with annuities, which are contracts written for a specific individual. Second, these bonds could be sold back like any other bond, while annuities are subject to high surrender charges, so individuals who realize they have accumulated too much can go back on their decision. Third, if the owner of a retirement bond dies before the term of the fixed period, the bond will be passed to heirs, who have the option to keep receiving the income or to sell the bond. This feature addresses what is a major brake on the purchase of annuities, namely the fact that individuals fear that they make a poor deal if they die earlier than expected, leaving most of the premium to the insurer.

Retirement bonds play a key role in the rest of this Element, as a liquid asset that allows future retirees to secure replacement income when they need it. As a result, we will look both at strategies in which they are held in isolation to purchase income, and at rebalanced strategies in which they are bought and sold to reduce uncertainty over the future replacement income.

3.4.4 Retirement Bonds as the Solution to the Decumulation Problem

Let us now return to the problem of spending retirement savings by withdrawing a fixed or cost-of-living-adjusted amount every year from the account. This encompasses two subquestions:

1. What is the maximum amount that can be withdrawn every year?
2. What investment strategy supports this fixed withdrawal without leading to a deficit in some scenarios?

As we show in Appendix A.3, the strategy is to invest savings in the retirement bond, and the maximum annual withdrawal is the value of savings at the beginning of decumulation, divided by the price of the retirement bond. Recall that the cash flows of the bond are normalized to $1 per year, plus possibly a cost-of-living adjustment.

This result answers the question of finding the optimal spending rate: it is the reciprocal of the retirement bond price. It also shows that to sustain this optimal spending for the duration of the decumulation period, savings must remain invested in the retirement bond price. As a consequence, any other investment strategy will require adjustments to consumption in response to changes in wealth.

4 Retirement Bonds and Their Usage

The previous section introduced retirement bonds as financial securities that produce stable replacement income for a predefined period, thereby matching the cash flow needs of individuals who retire at the beginning of the payment period. Bonds with these characteristics are currently not issued by the traditional issuers of high grade bonds, namely sovereign states and big corporations, so this section describes in detail the characteristics that they should ideally have, and it explains how to calculate their price by using observed bond prices and invoking no-arbitrage arguments. In the absence of these bonds in financial markets, a replicating portfolio – typically invested in regular bonds and other interest rate products – should be used as a substitute.

4.1 A Cash-Flow Matching Asset

The cash-flow schedule of a retirement bond is shown in Figure 5. As explained in Section 3.4, this bond has common features compared with a deferred annuity – namely the fact that income starts at the retirement date chosen by the

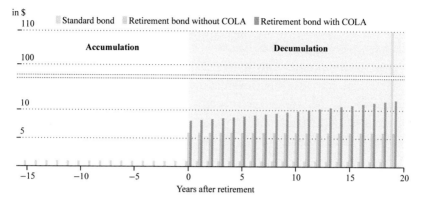

Figure 6 Cash flows of a retirement bond with or without cost-of-living adjustment and a standard coupon-paying bond.

Notes: For the purpose of illustration, it is assumed that all bonds have the same term, 20 years after retirement leave, and that the standard bond pays annual coupons. The standard bond has a face value of $100 and a coupon rate of 1%. The retirement bond without a cost-of-living adjustment (COLA) pays an annual cash flow of $6 for 20 years, beginning at the retirement date, and the retirement bond with a COLA pays an annual cash flow of $6, increasing by 2% per year. The reference date for the COLA is 15 years before retirement, so the first cash flow of the adjusted retirement bond is $6 \times 1.02^{15} = \$8.08$. The sum of cash flows for the standard bond and the retirement bond without a COLA over the period shown is $120.

individual and the fact that it is stable over time. The main differences between a bond and an annuity lie in their liquidity and reversibility. Being a security that yields fixed income for a predetermined period, a retirement bond is a sort of fixed-income instrument, but there are differences with respect to standard coupon-paying bonds, whether issued by Governments or by corporations.

Figure 6 shows the cash flows of two retirement bonds and a typical Government bond purchased 15 years before retirement. The two retirement bonds deliver cash flow on the same dates, and they only differ through the values of these cash flows, which are determined by the presence or the absence of a *cost-of-living adjustment* (COLA), which is described in detail as follows. Figure 6 highlights three key differences between a retirement bond and a standard bond, which are analyzed herein.

4.1.1 A Deferred Starting Date

A retirement bond has a deferred starting date for payments, while the ordinary bond starts to pay coupons to the owner right after the purchase date. But the individual does not need these income cash flows until he/she retires, because he/she has other sources of income including labor earnings, so he/she must reinvest these payments. The coupons are known ex ante, but the reinvestment rates are not, so the annual income generated by this strategy is not known until retirement, when accrued savings are annuitized by investing them in the bond. The reason for this uncertainty is not that the value of savings at retirement is unknown, but that the relative return of savings with respect to the bond over the accumulation period is unknown because of the coupon reinvestment. Thus, while purchasing a "fixed-income" product, the individual is still uncertain of the retirement income that he/she will eventually receive.

4.1.2 A Smooth Income Stream

The second difference between the two securities is that a retirement bond has no principal repayment at maturity, while the standard bond pays small cash flows (the coupons) until maturity and then a big lump sum (the principal plus the last coupon) at maturity. This difference originates in the fact that a retirement bond spreads interest payment and principal redemption over time in such a way that the annuity is constant. This amortization method should be familiar to households, as it is the dominant form of mortgage repayment: every period (usually, every month), the borrower repays some portion of capital and pays interest, but the sum of the two is constant. With this amortization scheme, individuals can rely both on interests and capital amortization to sustain their spending objectives, while in a low interest-rate environment, interests alone would not cover their needs.

4.1.3 Possibility of a Cost-of-Living Adjustment

The most standard form of coupon-paying bonds has principal and coupons fixed in nominal terms. Inflation-indexed securities exist, but they account for a minor share of outstanding Government bonds. For instance, on December 31, 2018, the US debt comprised $1.412 trillion in the form of Treasury inflation-protected securities (TIPS), versus $9.297 trillion in the form of Treasury notes, for a total marketable debt of $15.618 trillion.[18] In France, the amount of outstanding OAT (*Obligations Assimilables du Trésor*, which are nominal bonds) in October 2018 was €1,590 billion, versus €64 billion of OATi (bonds with principal linked to French price index) and €147 billion of OAT€i (bonds indexed on Eurozone price index).[19] So, indexed bonds represent some 9.0% of marketable debt in the US and 11.7% of outstanding bonds in France. They make up for a larger share of UK debt, where index-linked gilts amounted to

---

[18] Source: Monthly Statement of the Public Debt in December 2018, www.treasurydirect.gov/govt/reports/pd/mspd/mspd.htm.

[19] Source: Agence France Trésor, Key Figures for OATs, OATis and OAT€is, www.aft.gouv.fr.

£434 billion in December 2018, out of a total of £1,608 billion of outstanding gilt, and hence a percentage of 27%.[20] Retirement bonds can be of either type: income can be fixed in nominal terms, or proportional to realized inflation. In addition, a mid-term exists with a bond whose cash flows grow at a fixed annual rate proxying for expected inflation. This *cost-of-living adjustment* (COLA) does not exactly compensate an investor for increases in prices, but it at least reduces the impact of inflation on the purchasing power of replacement income.

With a COLA, the cash flows of the retirement bond have the increasing pattern shown in Figure 6. For the purpose of illustration, the annual growth rate in payments was set to 2% per year, a value that proxies for long-term expected inflation, and the reference date for indexation was taken to be the retirement date minus 15 years. Then, cash flows are constant in "real" terms, where the real value of a cash flow occurring n years after the reference date is defined here as the nominal value divided by 1.02^n. For instance, the first cash flow is paid at the retirement date, and hence 15 years after the reference date. Its real value in the illustration is $6, so its nominal value is

$$6 \times 1.02^{15} = \$8.08.$$

The reference date is equivalent to the "dated date" for TIPS in the US and OATi or OAT€i in France, which is the date at which inflation begins to accrue.

The distinction between nominal and real cash flows for bonds with a COLA can also be stated in terms of "current dollars" versus "constant dollars." The nominal value is the value in current dollars (i.e. the dollars of the date the cash flow is paid), and the real value is the value in dollars of the reference date. Formally, let t_0 denote the reference date and t the current date, the time scale being chosen in such a way that $t - t_0$ is the number of years elapsed between the two dates, and let π denotes the annual growth rate. $1 of date t_0 is equivalent to $\$[1 + \pi]^{t-t_0}$ of date t_0, so if y_t is the value in current dollars of a cash flow occurring at date t, its value in dollars of date t_0 is $y_t/[1 + \pi]^{t-t_0}$. It is less than y_t because $1 can purchase less at date t than at date t_0. The purpose of a COLA is to keep the value of income cash flows in dollars of the reference date constant, so the income cash flow for date t in current dollars must be

$$y_t = y_{t_0} \times [1 + \pi]^{t-t_0}. \tag{4.1}$$

In practice, the COLA can be taken equal to long-term expected inflation. Under the assumption of rational expectations, this ensures that the growth

---

[20] Source: United Kingdom Debt Management Office, Gilts in issue on 31 December 2018, www.dmo.gov.uk/data/.

in cash flows is in line with realized inflation in the long run. At finite horizons, there may be discrepancies between expected and realized inflation, but in developed economies with low inflation surprises, these should be limited. By this criterion, a value of 2% is a suitable choice both in the European Monetary Union and in the United States, because it happens to be the inflation target for the European Central Bank and the Federal Reserve, as per the following statements:

> "Price stability is defined as a year-on-year increase in the Harmonised Index of Consumer Prices (HICP) for the euro area of below 2%. Price stability is to be maintained over the medium term." Today, the Governing Council confirmed this definition (which it announced in 1998). At the same time, the Governing Council agreed that in the pursuit of price stability it will aim to maintain inflation rates close to **2%** over the medium term. This clarification underlines the ECB's commitment to provide a sufficient safety margin to guard against the risks of deflation.[21]

> The inflation rate over the longer run is primarily determined by monetary policy, and hence the Committee has the ability to specify a longer-run goal for inflation. The Committee judges that inflation at the rate of **2 percent**, as measured by the annual change in the price index for personal consumption expenditures, is most consistent over the longer run with the Federal Reserve's statutory mandate. Communicating this inflation goal clearly to the public helps keep longer-term inflation expectations firmly anchored, thereby fostering price stability and moderate long-term interest rates and enhancing the Committee's ability to promote maximum employment in the face of significant economic disturbances.[22]

4.2 Pricing Retirement Bonds

4.2.1 Retirement Bond as a Basket of Zero-Coupon Bonds

Because retirement bonds are not currently issued, they do not have an observable market price, unlike Government and corporate bonds. But one can still calculate a price "consistent" with existing bond quotes – that is, a "no-arbitrage" price. By definition, the no-arbitrage price of a security is the price at which it should trade to rule out the arbitrage opportunities that would be created if it was possible to replicate the cash flows of this security at a cost greater or less than the market price. It can be complex to calculate in the case

---

[21] Quoted from ECB's press release of May 8, 2003, entitled "The ECB's Monetary Policy Strategy". Available at www.ecb.europa.eu/press/pr/date/2003/html/pr030508_2.en.html. Emphasis is ours.

[22] Quoted from press release of January 25, 2012, entitled "Federal Reserve Issues FOMC Statement of Longer-Run Goals and Policy Strategy." Available at www.federalreserve.gov/newsevents/pressreleases/monetary20120125c.htm. Emphasis is ours.

of securities with non-linear exposures to risk factors, such as options, but for fixed-income instruments, the standard procedure is straightforward: the security is regarded as a basket of zero-coupon bonds with laddered maturity dates, each of which pays one of the cash flows, and the no-arbitrage price is the sum of the zero-coupon bond prices.

A representation of a multi-cash-flow bond as a basket of zero-coupon bonds is provided by Figure 6. For a retirement bond, there is one cash flow per period, so the maturity dates of the zero-coupon instruments are selected dates in the periods. In what follows, we will assume that cash flows are annual and that the payment date is the first day in the year that is not a Saturday or a Sunday, but this is nothing but a convention, and the pricing procedure can accommodate other rules, like end-of-period payments and monthly cash flows.

The price of a retirement bond is clearly proportional to the constant income level in the case of a bond with no COLA, and to the income level in constant dollars in the case of a bond with a COLA. So, without loss of generality, one can price the bond under the assumption that income is $1 per year, and simply scale down or up the price thus obtained to get the price for an arbitrary income level. In the remainder of this Element, we let β_t denote the price at date t of a retirement bond with unit cash flows.

4.2.2 Mathematical Formula

To write a mathematical expression for β_t, a few symbols are needed. T denotes the retirement date, and τ is the duration of the decumulation period, say 20 years, assuming a 20-year life expectancy at retirement age. The time scale is chosen in such a way that the difference between two dates s and t, $t - s$, represents the fractional number of years between these dates. The annual growth rate that applies to cash flows is π, and the reference date for indexation is t_0.

The bond pays τ cash flows starting at date T, with an annual frequency, so the cash flows take place at dates $T, T+1, \ldots, T+\tau-1$. The income cash flow at date s is $[1 + \pi]^{s-t_0}$ in dollars of date s, which is equivalent to 1 in dollars of date t_0. The discount factor that applies to a cash flow of date s is $b_{t,s}$, the price at date t of a zero-coupon bond maturing at date s and having a unit face value. The retirement bond price at date t is thus

$$\beta_t = \sum_{s=T}^{T+\tau-1} [1 + \pi]^{s-t_0} \times b_{t,s}. \qquad (4.2)$$

This quantity is the price to pay at date t to purchase $1 of replacement income per year for τ years beginning at retirement date. The annual dollar of income is expressed in dollars of date t_0. By setting π to zero, we recover the price of a

bond without a COLA, and the result is of course independent from the choice
of any reference date t_0. To alleviate the notation, we do not explicitly indicate
the dependence of β_t with respect to the retirement date (T), the decumulation
period (τ) and the growth rate (π), but it should be kept in mind that all these
parameters have an impact.

The price of a zero-coupon bond with maturity $s - t$ can be written as

$$b_{t,s} = \exp\left(-[s - t]y_{t,s-t}\right), \tag{4.3}$$

where $y_{t,s-t}$ is the continuously compounded zero-coupon rate of maturity $s - t$
prevailing at date t. Because the cash flows are fixed, the discount rates to use
are *nominal* rates, so we need a nominal zero-coupon curve to price a retirement
bond. The next section describes methods to obtain a zero-coupon curve.

Equations (4.2) and (4.3) make it clear that the price of a retirement bond
depends on the zero-coupon yield curve, in addition to the retirement date, the
length of the decumulation period, the COLA and the reference indexation date.
Like a standard bond price, it is decreasing in the level of interest rates, and in
the bond maturity: the longer the time to retirement, the lower the bond price.

4.2.3 Obtaining Zero-Coupon Rates Series

Zero-coupon bonds are not as widely traded as coupon-paying bonds, so that
the usual approach is to start from the market quotes of actively traded bonds
and to infer the prices of fictitious zero-coupon instruments that have generated
the observed quotes. As a result, zero-coupon rates are estimated rather than
observed.

A number of mathematical methods are available to estimate zero-coupon
rates from market bond quotes. Martellini, Priaulet and Priaulet (2003) describe
in detail, and provide empirical examples for, bootstrapping, the exponential
splines of Vasicek and Fong (1982), the polynominal splines of McCulloch
(1971) and McCulloch (1975), and the model of Nelson and Siegel (1987) and
Svensson (1994), which is described in detail in what follows. The general
approach in all these methods is to reduce the continuous yield curve – which
has in theory infinitely many points because the yield maturity can take on any
value – to a finite number of parameters, and to estimate parameters by running
a non-linear regression, that is by minimizing the magnitude of the differences
between the model-implied bond prices and the market quotes. Before minimizing the pricing errors, one has to specify a set of securities on which the
model will be calibrated, by focusing on sufficiently liquid bonds and avoiding those with embedded options, which cannot be decomposed as a basket of
zero-coupon bonds. Martellini, Priaulet and Priaulet (2003, p. 96–97), discuss
selection criteria.

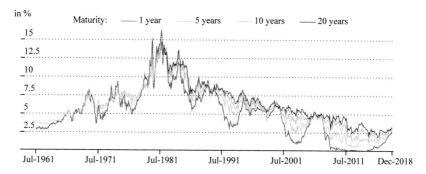

Figure 7 US zero-coupon rates, 1961 to 2019.

In the US, Gürkaynak, Sack and Wright (2007) estimate a Nelson-Siegel model for the period from June 6, 1961, to January 1, 1980, and a Nelson-Siegel-Svensson model, which is an extended form of the Nelson-Siegel representation of zero-coupon rates, for the period from January 2, 1980, to current date. Their output dataset contains the parameter estimates and time series of zero-coupon rates for the maturities from 1 to 7, 10, 15, 20 or 30 years, depending on the period. For instance, rates of maturities ranging from 20 to 30 years are available as of November 1985, because the Treasury Department began the issuance of 30-year bonds only in 1985. The dataset is periodically updated and is available on the website of the Federal Reserve. Figure 7 shows a sample of zero-coupon rates from this dataset: they exhibited a decreasing trend from 1981 to 2017, and the 1-year rate almost fell to zero after 2011 and the Fed's decision to set its Federal Funds Rate to historically low levels in response to the liquidity crisis.

In other countries, zero-coupon rates may also be available, but the coverage in terms of available maturities and sample length is not as extensive as in the US. In the UK, zero-coupon rates of maturities 5, 10 and 20 years are published on the website of the Bank of England. The documentation indicates that they are obtained through a spline method developed by Waggoner (1997).[23] In France, the Comité de Normalisation Obligataire (French Bond Association) calculates zero-coupon rates for the maturities from 1 to 60 year(s), by using Euribor futures contracts at the short end of the yield curve, and interest rate swaps for longer maturities.[24] Table 1 summarizes the availability of zero-coupon rates series in the US, the UK and France. This list is restricted

---

[23] The methodology for the calculation of UK zero-coupon rates is presented by Anderson and Sleath (2001).

[24] Detailed methodology is exposed in CNO/FBA (2015). On p. 5, the short end of the curve is defined as the portion "up to two or three year[s]." The calculation procedure combines bootstrapping and cubic interpolation.

Table 1 Availability of zero-coupon rate series from public and free sources.

Country	Source	Data frequency	Maturities (years)	Start date
United States	Federal Reserve*	Daily	1–7	1961-06-14
			8–10	1971-08-16
			11–15	1971-11-15
			16–20	1981-07-20
			21–30	1985-11-25
United Kingdom	Bank of England**	Daily	5, 10	1982-01-04
			20	1992-02-11
France	Comité de Normalisation Obligataire (French Bond Association)***	Monthly	1–60	2011-29-02

Notes: *: www.federalreserve.gov/pubs/feds/2006/200628/200628abs.html.
**: www.bankofengland.co.uk/boeapps/iadb.
***: www.cnofrance.org/fr/courbes-des-taux-zero-coupon.cfm.

to public and free sources, and thus excludes commercial data providers, though they may also provide such series.

4.2.4 Filling Gaps in the Term Structure

The maturities of the zero-coupon rates given in the datasets are integer numbers, but for the purpose of pricing the retirement bond at any date, non-integer maturities are also needed, since cash flows do not always occur within a round number of years from the pricing date. Linear interpolation between the nearest two integer maturities is an easy way to fill in the gaps in the term structure, and higher-order methods, like quadratic and cubic interpolation, can also be used. In the special case where the term structure is generated by a Nelson-Siegel or a Nelson-Siegel-Svensson model, as described in Appendix B.1, the rate of any maturity can be directly obtained by applying a calculation formula that takes the parameter estimates and the given maturity as inputs (Equation (B.1) in the Appendix).

More problematic is the question of extrapolation outside the range of available maturities. In a retirement bond pricing exercise, the need for long maturity rates can quickly arise, owing to the long duration of the decumulation period. For instance, if decumulation is 20 years long and cash flows are paid at the beginning of each period, the longest cash flow occurs 19 years after retirement, then calculating the bond price at the retirement date requires rates of maturities up to 19 years. To calculate the price 10 years before retirement, the longest maturity needed is 29 years, and at any point in the accumulation phase, it will be the sum of the time to retirement and the length of the decumulation period, here 20 years. On the other hand, zero-coupon rates are provided up to a certain maturity, which is in fact determined by the longest maturity of the securities or contracts on which the estimation procedure of the yield curve is based. In the US, the longest maturity for a Treasury bond at auction is currently 30 years, so no bond longer than 30 years can be found at any point in time. Because the estimation method of Gürkaynak, Sack and Wright (2007) uses Treasury quotes, the maximum maturity for zero-coupon rates is therefore 30 years. The CNO method for France uses interest rate swaps, which exist for longer maturities, so zero-coupon rates can be calculated up to 60 years.

In case the bond pricing exercise requires rates with maturities exceeding the longest maturity provided in the dataset, an easy solution is to assume a flat term structure beyond this point. This approach should, however, be used with caution because it assigns an arbitrary price to cash flows that occur far ahead in the future, and it does not recognize that the market does not give them a price.

4.3 Retirement Bond Price and Classification of Goals in Retirement Investing

The retirement bond price is a useful piece of information in itself because it allows to measure the purchasing power of savings in terms of replacement income. As a result, an investor accumulating money for retirement can know whether his/her savings are sufficient to generate the income amount that he/she targets. This section explains how retirement income objectives can be classified as *affordable* or *aspirational*.

4.3.1 Measuring the Purchasing Power of Savings in Terms of Replacement Income

As explained previously, the retirement bond price is determined by the retirement date, the duration of the decumulation period, the COLA and the reference indexation date, and it depends on time through the discount rates. For any combination of the first four parameters, the price to pay at date t to acquire \$1 of replacement income every year is β_t, so the annual replacement income that an investor endowed with capital W_t at date t can purchase is

$$ri_t = \frac{W_t}{\beta_t}. \tag{4.4}$$

With a zero COLA, dollars of all dates are considered equivalent, so the replacement income can be indifferently expressed in dollars of any date. If a non-zero COLA is applied, with a reference date t_0, the bond cash flows are normalized to \$1 of date t_0 per year, so the quantity in Equation (4.4) is the number of dollars of date t_0 that an investor endowed with savings W_t can acquire. Because \$1 of date t_0 is equivalent to $\$[1 + \pi]^{t-t_0}$ of date t, the replacement income expressed in dollars of date t is

$$ri_t^{(t)} = ri_t^{(t_0)} \times [1 + \pi]^{t-t_0},$$

where the superscript t or t_0 denotes the date of the dollars and $ri_t^{(t_0)}$ is the value in Equation (4.4). Interestingly, the replacement income in dollars of date t can be rewritten without a reference to date t_0, since the effects of t_0 on $ri_t^{(t_0)}$ and $[1 + \pi]^{t-t_0}$ cancel out. To see this, rewrite it as

$$ri_t^{(t)} = \frac{W_t}{\displaystyle\sum_{s=T}^{T+\tau-1} [1 + \pi]^{s-t} b_{t,s}}.$$

The purchasing power on a given date, as given by Equation (4.4), is known at this date because it depends on the current value of savings, which are observable, and the current retirement bond price, which is a function of observable parameters (the retirement date, the duration of the decumulation period, the COLA and the reference indexation date) and of current interest rates. But the future values of the purchasing power are unknown for two reasons:

- The future values of savings are unknown because they depend on the contributions that the individual will make to his/her savings account and on how his/her portfolio will perform.
- The future retirement bond prices are unknown because they depend on future interest rate conditions.

In the language of probabilities, the future values of the purchasing power are *random variables*.

That said, there is a situation in which they are certain as opposed to being random: if the individual does not plan to make any new contribution in the future *and* his/her portfolio is entirely invested in the retirement bond. Under these two conditions, the performance of the savings account exactly replicates that of the retirement bond, so that the amount of income that savings can finance is constant over time. But for arbitrary contribution schedules and other investment choices, the relative returns of the savings account with respect to the retirement bond fluctuate, so the levels of purchasing power attained in the future are uncertain.

4.3.2 Goals in Retirement Investing

In retirement investing, the objective is to generate replacement income, so a goal is naturally defined as a level of income that the individual would like to sustain for the first τ years of retirement. The first question that arises is whether a goal is "attainable" or not. Until he/she retires, an individual does not know how much income his/her pension pot can finance for the aforementioned reasons. He/she only knows how much income his/her current savings can purchase, by dividing them by the retirement bond price (Equation (4.4)).

In the terminology introduced by Deguest et al. (2015), the purchasing power of savings at a given point in time is the *maximum affordable income level* at this date because it is the maximum income level that the investor can secure with current savings. This level is effectively secured by investing savings in the retirement bond. Higher levels can be attained by the retirement date if the performance of the savings account exceeds that of the retirement bond. There are two decisions that an individual can make to achieve these higher goals, and they can be used jointly:

- Bring fresh money in the form of additional contributions (i.e. save more).
- Choose a portfolio strategy that has the potential to outperform the retirement bond.

Future contributions are hypothetical in nature, and so are the future returns on a portfolio with respect to the retirement bond, unless the portfolio is entirely invested in the bond itself, so that income levels greater than the maximum affordable level cannot be reached with certainty. In the language of goal-based investing, they are said to be *aspirational goals*, and one challenge for a goal-based investing strategy is precisely to deliver as high probabilities of reaching them as possible.

In contrast, any income level less than or equal to the maximum affordable level is said to be an *affordable goal* because the individual can secure it by investing his/her savings in the retirement bond. In fact, if the targeted level is strictly less than the maximum, it suffices for the individual to invest less than current savings in the bond. Formally, if the target ri_{tar} is less than ri_t, the amount to invest in the retirement bond is $ri_{tar} \times \beta_t$, which is less than W_t. The income level to secure is referred to as the *essential goal*: any affordable goal can serve as an essential goal.

4.3.3 Why Set an Essential Goal That Is Less Than the Maximum Affordable Level?

As explained in detail in Section 5, the motivation to decide to secure less than the maximum possible is to keep money available for investing in assets that have the potential to outperform the retirement bond, like equities. With the previous notations, if an individual decides to secure ri_{min} instead of ri_t, he/she can do so by investing $ri_{min} \times \beta_t$ in the retirement bond, which leaves an amount

$$W_t - ri_{min} \times \beta_t = [ri_t - ri_{min}] \beta_t$$

available for investing in equities.

Let T be the retirement date and assume that no contribution takes place between dates t and T, and denote with $R_{equ,t,T}$ the gross return on equities over this period. Then, the value of savings at the retirement date is

$$W_T = ri_{min}\beta_T + [W_t - ri_{min}\beta_t] R_{equ,t,T}, \tag{4.5}$$

and the purchasing power of savings is W_T/β_T. Simple algebraic manipulation shows that the difference between the change in the purchasing power from date t to date T is

$$ri_T - ri_t = [ri_t - ri_{min}] \times \left[\frac{\beta_t}{\beta_T} R_{equ,t,T} - 1 \right]. \tag{4.6}$$

It follows from Equation (4.6) that if the individual sets an essential goal at the maximum level ($ri_t = ri_{min}$) and does not make a new contribution by retirement, the purchasing power is unchanged. If he/she sets an essential goal less than the maximum, then the purchasing power of savings increases if, and only if, the equity portfolio outperforms the retirement bond. To have a chance (i.e. a non-zero probability) of reaching an income level greater than the maximum affordable level, the investor must fulfill two conditions: set an essential goal strictly lower than the current maximum affordable level (i.e. secure less than what is feasible) and invest in an asset that has the potential to outperform the retirement bond. Here, this asset is taken to be an equity portfolio, but it can be any asset, as long as this asset outperforms the bond with positive probability.

In the absence of arbitrage opportunities, it is impossible to find an asset that outperforms the retirement bond with 100% probability, so there is a non-zero probability for the investor of ending up with less purchasing power than at date t. This is the price to pay to have also a non-zero probability of seeing an increase in the purchasing power. In other words, reaching an aspirational goal, defined as a non-affordable goal, requires some *risk taking*, where risk is defined here as the risk of losing purchasing power in the future with respect to the current situation.[25] Thus, risk is understood here as *downside risk* for the value of savings with respect to the retirement bond.

It should be noted that downside risk is limited in size, because we have, by Equation (4.5),

$$ri_T - ri_{min} = \frac{W_t - ri_{min}\beta_t}{\beta_T}R_{equ,t,T},$$

which is a positive quantity. So, the eventually affordable income level is greater than ri_{min}.

This strategy – take buy-and-hold positions in the retirement bond and an equity portfolio – is an elementary example of *goal-based investing strategies*, which are designed to protect an essential goal while having the potential to reach aspirational goals. Other examples will be presented in Section 6.

4.3.4 Numerical Examples

Consider a US investor planning to retire in January 2009. Figure 8 shows the price of retirement bonds with or without a COLA from January 1999 through January 2019, which is the end of the dataset at the time this Element is being written. The start date was taken to be the retirement date minus 11 years, so that the maturity of the last income cash flow, paid in January 2028, does not

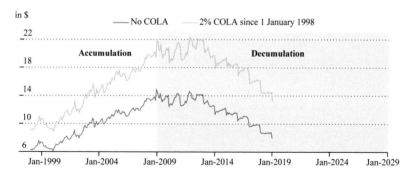

Figure 8 Retirement bond prices for a US investor retiring in January 2009, 1999 to 2019.

Notes: The investor plans to retire on January 1, 2009. The "No COLA" line shows the price of the retirement bond when no COLA is required, and the other line represents the price when a COLA is applied as a 2% annual growth rate in income cash flows. The reference date for indexation for the latter bond is January 1, 1998. The decumulation period is 20 years long, and prices are calculated until the end of the dataset, in January 2019.

---

[25] Another option to increase the purchasing power of savings, not considered here, is to make new contributions by retirement.

exceed 30 years, which is the maturity of the longest zero-coupon rate available in the dataset. In the presence of a COLA, the reference date for indexation is January 1, 1998, so the first cash flow, which is paid on January 11, 2009, is

$$1 \times 1.02^{11} = \$1.2434.$$

Cash flows then grow by 2% every year until January 2028. Because they are greater in nominal value than \$1, the bond price is greater than without a COLA.

During the accumulation phase, bond prices increase because of two effects. First, the cash flow maturities decrease, so the discount factors increase, and second, interest rates were decreasing in this period, which inflates the discount rates. As a result, bond prices peak near the retirement date. In the decumulation period, \$1 cash flows are paid every year beginning in January 2009. Price is discontinuous on the cash flow dates, and these downward jumps clearly appear on the plot.

The variation in the bond price shown in Figure 8 is the result of two causes, namely the passage of time and changes in interest rates. To isolate the effect of the second factor, we plot in Figure 9 the price of the retirement bond by keeping the time to retirement fixed. This allows us to compare the purchasing powers in terms of income of two individuals who plan to retire in the same amount of time but arrive at different dates. Calculations begin in January 1986 to ensure that discount rates of maturities longer than 20 years are available (see Table 1). For retirement horizons of 5 and 10 years, the longest cash flow maturities are, respectively, 25 and 30 years, so no extrapolation beyond the 30-year maturity is needed, but for the 20-year horizon, rates of maturities ranging from 31 to 40 years are required, while the longest available maturity is 30 years. Then,

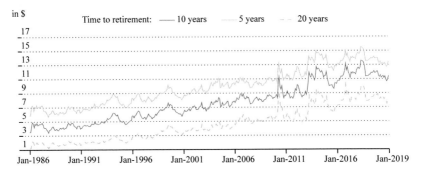

Figure 9 Retirement bond prices for a US investor and a fixed time to retirement, 1986 to 2019.

Notes: The retirement bond price is calculated on each date of the horizontal axis, for an investor retiring 5, 10 or 20 years after this date. The decumulation period is 20 years long, and no COLA is applied to income cash flows.

the pricing of the retirement bond involves extrapolation of the 30-year rate beyond the 30-year maturity.

Figure 9 shows that the price of $1 of replacement income per year increased significantly between 1986 and 2019, as a consequence of decreasing interest rates, and the increase is bigger for longer retirement horizons: for horizons of 5, 10 and 20 years, the price was multiplied respectively by 2.28, 3.27 and 6.84. Indeed, a longer time to retirement implies longer cash flow maturities and hence a greater sensitivity to interest rate changes, like for standard bonds: it is well known that long-term bonds have higher exposure to interest rate risk than short-term bonds because of their longer duration. In January 1986, an individual planning to retire in 10 years, and thus in 1996, had to spend $3.5 to acquire $1 of replacement income per year. In 2019, it cost $11.44 for an investor with the same horizon to purchase the same stream of income.

Put differently, the purchasing power of fixed capital in terms of income decreased between 1986 and 2019. Figure 10 shows the income level that a US investor retiring in 10 years could purchase with $100,000. By definition, any level below the curve is an "affordable goal" because it can be secured with the $100,000, while any level above is an "aspirational goal" because it cannot be secured and requires some risk taking to be reached with a non-zero probability, as explained in Section 4.3. In January 1986, $100,000 in savings could purchase an income stream of $28,546 per year starting in 1996. With $100,000 in January 2019, the same income level has become an aspirational goal, 3.27 times as large as the maximum affordable level of $8,736 per year.

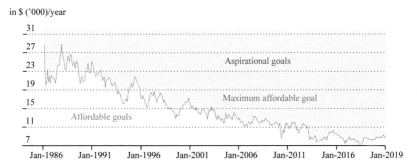

Figure 10 Purchasing power of $100,000 in terms of replacement income for a US investor planning to retire in 10 years, 1986 to 2019.
Notes: The line is the amount of replacement income, starting 10 years after the date on the horizontal axis and lasting for 20 years, that can be purchased with $100,000. No COLA is applied to income cash flows. Any income level less than or equal to the amount that can be financed with $100,000 is said to be an "affordable goal," and any income level greater than the maximum is said to be an "aspirational goal."

4.4 How to Secure Replacement Income (or Fail To)

4.4.1 The Retirement Bond as an Accumulation and a Decumulation Tool

The retirement bond is the safe asset for an individual wanting to generate a fixed income stream for a predefined period from his/her savings. It is both an accumulation and a decumulation product. In the accumulation phase, it can be used to secure the purchasing power of savings in terms of income. In decumulation, it solves the decumulation problem exposed in Section 3 by ensuring that savings are efficiently consumed. Indeed, at the time of retirement, the individual knows the purchasing power of his/her savings in terms of replacement income, given by Equation (4.4). Provided he/she withdraws this exact amount from his/her savings account at the start of every year, the account balance will be exactly zero at the end of the decumulation period. This means that savings last for the entire period and that no surplus is left at the end, so that the individual enjoys the highest possible consumption level every year without facing the risk of running short of resources before the term.

In accumulation, the retirement bond allows an investor to build up a pension pot by incrementing the purchasing power in terms of future replacement income by a known amount every time a contribution is made. Each contribution has a certain purchasing power in terms of income, which is known at the time money is brought in: it is equal to the amount of money brought by the individual, divided by the retirement bond price at this date. The purchasing power attained at retirement is the sum of all past increments. It is not known until the last contribution is made for two reasons: future contributions are uncertain by nature, and the purchasing power of a dollar brought during the accumulation phase is not known because it depends on the retirement bond price on the date the contribution is made.

4.4.2 A Case Study

Consider two US investors who both plan to retire on January 1, 2009, but differ through their contribution schedule. The first invests $10,000 in January 1998 and does not bring new money thereafter, while the second brings $10,000 at the beginning of every year from 1998 through 2008, the year before retirement. The annual contributions are assumed to grow at 3% per year, so as to reflect an increase in investor's labor earnings or a more pronounced savings effort as retirement approaches: the 2009 contribution is $10,300, the 2010 one is $10,609 and so on.

The balance of the savings account at any point in the accumulation or the decumulation phase depends on contributions and withdrawals made so far and the performance of the fund(s) in which savings are invested. In general, there can be multiple funds – for example, if the individual invests the different contributions in different supports. Mathematical expressions are given in Appendix B.2.

Panel (a) in Figure 11 shows the simulated wealth of each individual, and Panel (b) displays the purchasing power of their savings in terms of replacement income, with a 2% annual COLA. It clearly appears that when savings are fully invested in the retirement bond, their purchasing power remains strictly constant, as long as the individual does not bring any new money. When regular

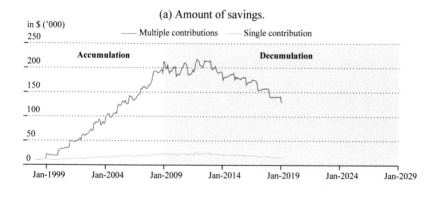

(a) Amount of savings.

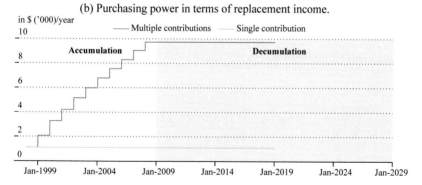

(b) Purchasing power in terms of replacement income.

Figure 11 Simulation of the situation of US individuals investing in the retirement bond and making a single contribution or annual contributions, 1998 to 2019.

Notes: Both investors plan to retire on January 1, 2009, and bring $10,000 on January 1, 1998. One of them makes an additional contribution every year, starting at $10,000 in 1998 and growing by 3% per year. All contributions are fully invested in the retirement bond. In the decumulation phase, the annual withdrawal equals the maximum affordable income level at the retirement date. Panel (b) shows the purchasing power of accrued savings in terms of replacement income with a 2% COLA. Income is expressed in dollars as of January 1998.

savings are added, the purchasing power has a staircase pattern, where the height of a step is the marginal contribution of a cash infusion to the purchasing power of the pension pot. This height equals the contribution value divided by the retirement bond price on that date. In this example, heights tend to decrease over time, although the savings inflow increases by 3% per year, meaning that the increase in savings does not make up for the increase in the retirement bond price, shown in Figure 8.

By making additional savings every year, the first investor is eventually able to purchase a stream of 9,733 dollars of 1998 per year, beginning in January 2009. Because the annual COLA is 2%, the income cash flows expressed in current dollars are much higher than this. In January 2009, the amount of income received is

$$9,733 \times 1.02^{11} = \$12,102,$$

and the replacement income cash flows in current dollars are those shown in Figure 12. The other investor ends accumulation with a purchasing power of 1,106 dollars of 1998 per year.

In decumulation, both individuals keep investing in the retirement bond, and they spend the maximum amount permitted by their situation in January 2009 – that is, they withdraw every year the amount shown in Figure 12. These withdrawals imply a decreasing pattern for wealth, but they do not affect the purchasing power of wealth, which remains flat through the decumulation period. This property is formally proved in Appendix B.2.

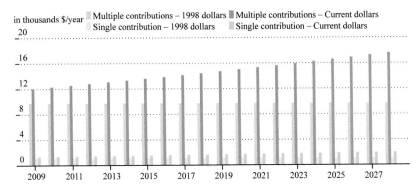

Figure 12 Replacement income cash flows for the individuals of Figure 11.
Notes: The individuals are those of Figure 11. The first makes annual contributions starting at $10,000 in January 1998 and growing by 3% per year until January 2008, and the second makes a single contribution of $10,000 in 1998. Both retire in January 2009, so the replacement income cash flows occur from January 2009 to January 2028. They grow at 2% per year.

4.4.3 Bad Substitutes for the Retirement Bond

Sovereign bonds and money market instruments are traditionally regarded as "safe" assets for different reasons. Standard sovereign bonds pay a fixed coupon every year or semester, unlike stocks, whose dividends fluctuate with firms' activity: thus, they are fixed-income products. For highly rated issuers, they are also credited for having very low default risk. Funds deposited in a cash account are rolled over at a short-term rate that can vary over time, but as long as it is nonnegative, the nominal value of savings never decreases. So, capital is protected, and the value of savings at retirement is at least equal to the sum of invested contributions.

In spite of these properties, they are not as "safe" as they look when it comes to generating income in retirement. Figure 6 shows that the cash-flow schedule of a standard coupon-paying bond is very different from the cash flows needed by an individual. The bond pays coupons during accumulation, while an individual preparing for retirement does not need replacement income until he/she retires, and in decumulation, the bond pays unequal cash flows, dominated by the principal repayment at maturity, while a retiree expects stable cash flows. One can avoid the maturity effect by selling a bond before it matures and replacing it with a new bond. Such a rollover strategy is implemented in bond indices like the US Treasury index considered in Figure 4, but by following it, an individual does not know at the start of decumulation how much he/she can safely withdraw every year without exhausting savings before the end of the period and without leaving an unnecessary final surplus.

Investing in cash has the same shortcoming, since Figure 4 shows that the withdrawal rate is not known in advance. In accumulation, an individual who saves in cash knows that he/she will retire with at least the sum of invested contributions in the pension pot, but he/she does not know what level of replacement income this amount of money can finance until he/she retires.

To see that the bond index and the cash account are not good substitutes for the retirement bond in accumulation, one can look at how the purchasing power of a capital invested in these two asset classes has evolved over time. With the retirement bond, this quantity is constant by definition, and if an asset is a valuable proxy for this asset, it should yield a stable purchasing power. Note that the gross change in the level of affordable income (Equation (4.4)) between two dates t and $t + h$ is given by

$$\frac{ri_{t+h}}{ri_t} = \frac{W_{t+h}}{W_t} \times \frac{\beta_t}{\beta_{t+h}}, \tag{4.7}$$

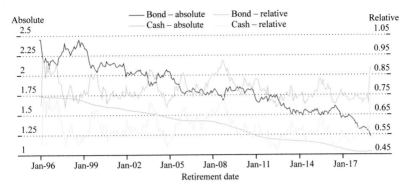

Figure 13 Absolute returns of bonds and cash and relative returns with respect to the retirement bond over the 10 years before retirement.

Notes: For each retirement date, the price of the retirement bond is calculated by discounting future cash flows. The left axis shows the absolute gross return of standard bonds, represented by the Barclays US Treasury index, and that of cash, represented by a daily rollover of 3-month US Treasury bills. The right axis shows the gross return of bonds or cash divided by the gross return of the retirement bond over the 10 years preceding the retirement date. A relative return less (resp., greater) than 100% indicates that the asset underperformed (resp., outperformed) the retirement bond.

so it is equal to the relative return of savings with respect to the retirement bond. We consider a rolling accumulation period of 20 years with a one-month shift in the retirement date from one period to the next.

As appears from Figure 13, the bond index and the cash account were far from stabilizing the purchasing power of savings in terms of replacement income during the various accumulation periods. It is only by accident that their relative returns equal 1, and for most periods, they are different from 1. In fact, they failed to preserve the purchasing power of savings in terms of retirement income for all the retirement dates shown here, as can be seen by noting that relative returns are always less than 1. Consider, for instance, an individual planning to retire in January 2018 and starting to accumulate in January 2008. If they had been invested in the bond index, the purchasing power of the savings would have decreased by 26.3% during these 10 years, and with cash, it would have fallen down by 45.1%. Both the bond index and cash did preserve the nominal value of savings in all accumulation periods, since their absolute return was greater than 1, although it exhibits a decreasing trend due to the decrease in interest rates that took place between 1986 and 2019. But in each period, the retirement bond price outperformed bonds and cash, so the individual was unable to finance as much income at the end compared to at the beginning of the period.

Because returns are highly sensitive to the choice of the sample period, this picture might look different in other market conditions – in particular if interest rates had been increasing as opposed to being decreasing. Indeed, increasing rates would have implied lower returns for the retirement bond, so the relative returns would have been possibly higher. Regardless of the peculiarities of the period at hand, an important conclusion from Figure 13 is that an individual who saves in a bond index or in a cash account faces substantial uncertainty over the evolution of the purchasing power of savings: for the bond index, 10-year relative returns ranged from 68.8% to 93.5%, and for cash, they ranged from 46.8% to 75.7%.

4.4.4 Goal-Hedging Portfolio

That is not to say that standard bonds and cash are useless in retirement invest-ment, but they are useful if they are used as *replicating instruments* for the retirement bond, which is the only asset that preserves the affordable income level across all market conditions. Thus, they can enter a *goal-hedging port-folio*, defined as a portfolio that replicates the returns of the retirement bond by combining fixed-income instruments. The construction of this portfolio is similar to that of the liability-hedging portfolio in asset-liability management, and standard weighting methods include matching of durations, matching of durations and convexities and matching of exposures to the level and the slope factors. But as such, a standard bond portfolio or a money market account can-not act as valuable goal-hedging portfolios because their durations do not match that of the retirement bond. The bond portfolio has a relatively stable duration over time, typically much shorter than that of the retirement bond during the accumulation phase, and a cash account has zero duration, so its returns do not mimic those of the retirement bond.

5 Improving Accumulation Products

During the pre-retirement phase, the investor's objective is to accumulate sav-ings that will be used in decumulation to generate replacement income. As explained herein, this justifies the focus on the purchasing power of savings in terms of replacement income, as opposed to the nominal value of savings.

In conventional financial advice, capital accumulation and income gener-ation are generally seen as two competing objectives, the former of which would be best reached by investing in equities and the latter by investing in bonds. As a result, the standard recommendation is for young investors to hold a greater fraction of equities, and for retired or close to retired individuals to favor bonds. This prescription is implemented in target date funds, which let the equity allocation progressively and automatically decrease as the target date approaches.

One can ask, however, if the objective to generate replacement income would not be better served by taking it into account earlier in the accumulation phase. As shown in Section 4, an individual who accumulates money in the retirement bond knows as soon as he/she brings new savings how much replacement income these savings will finance, while an investor who chooses a standard bond portfolio or a cash account faces substantial uncertainty over the level of income that he/she will eventually reach. In this section, we consider two popular forms of mutual funds, namely balanced funds and target date funds, and we study modified versions of these well-established products that use the retirement bond as a building block.

5.1 Balanced Funds and Target Date Funds

Balanced funds and target date funds are invested in asset classes with different risk-return profiles – mainly equities, bonds and cash. One important premise that determines the allocation rules of the various funds is that equities have higher long-term growth potential than bonds and cash, but that they expose investors to significant risk of capital loss in the short run, while cash preserves capital and sovereign and corporate bonds from highly rated issuers deliver stable and predictable cash flows. As a result, a fund dominated by equities is said to favor capital accumulation over income distribution, at the risk of short-term losses, while a fund mainly invested in bonds is said to favor income distribution and capital protection.

5.1.1 Conventional Financial Advice

Balanced funds seek to maintain a roughly constant percentage allocation to each of the asset classes that constitute them.[26] The "60/40" weighting rule, which recommends that 60% be invested in equities and the rest in bonds and cash, is a popular rule of thumb, but "aggressive" funds can allocate as much as 80% to equities, while "conservative" funds can allocate this percentage to bonds. However, the adjectives of "aggressive" and "conservative" do not refer to standard percentages of equities and bonds, and each provider has its own terminology.

---

[26] As recalled by Malkiel (1996, p. 368) and DeMiguel, Garlappi and Uppal (2009), this investment guideline dates back at least to the Babylonian Talmud, in which Rabbi Yitzhak recommended that "a person should always divide his money into three; he should bury one-third in the ground, and invest one-third in business, and keep one-third in his possession." (quoted from the William Davidson Talmud, Bava Mezia 42a).

In principle, an investor can pick an equity weight by deciding how much he/she is willing to accept to lose in the event of a bear equity market, or by deciding how frequent and how large swings in the value of his/her portfolio he/she is comfortable with. These two criteria correspond respectively to tolerance for loss risk and tolerance for volatility. But in practice, individual investors are not equipped with the datasets and the technical background needed to run simulations of savings with different equity allocations, so they must resort to conventional advice or rules of thumb to choose an allocation.

A number of such rules have been proposed, but it turns out that the horizon at which money is needed and the age are two criteria often cited as relevant when it comes to choosing a target allocation to equities. Broadly speaking, investors who have a longer horizon are generally advised to have a higher percentage of their savings invested in stocks because they have time to recover from short-term losses. On the other hand, those who plan to withdraw money in the short run are advised to overweight low-risk assets like bonds and money market funds. Similarly, retired investors, who need stable and regular income, are recommended larger allocations to bonds. Real estate is also sometimes cited as an asset that generates income and, as such, would be attractive for retirees.

If one acknowledges that a person's age should be an important driver of the equity allocation and that older investors should hold a higher percentage of bonds, then it makes sense to develop another class of funds, in which the equity allocation automatically decreases as time goes by. This investment policy is implemented in *target date funds*, which have a target date embedded in their name (e.g. the "2045 fund") and let the equity allocation be a decreasing function of the time to this date: the function that maps the horizon, defined as the distance between the target date and the current one, into the equity allocation is known as the *glidepath*. With these funds, investors do not need to readjust their portfolio by themselves.

5.1.2 Product Overview

Target date funds subdivide in "to" and "through" funds. A "to" fund is designed to take an investor *to* the target date, so the equity allocation decreases until that date, while a "through" fund takes the investor *through* the target date and allows the equity allocation continue to decrease after that point. "Through" funds generally allocate a greater fraction to equities than "to" funds before the target date. But the horizon is not the sole determinant of a fund's allocation, and there exist "conservative" and "aggressive" variants of these funds. Like for balanced funds, however, these adjectives have no standard meaning and they do not refer to specific percentages of equities, so that each provider uses them in a self-defined sense.

Balanced funds and target date funds are often funds of funds, meaning that they are invested in underlying funds, each of which is used to achieve exposure to a given category of assets. An underlying stock fund can represent a specific class of stocks, like large domestic, international, mid-cap, value, or companies that invest in "real assets" such as infrastructure, commodities and real estate. On the bond side, examples of categories include, among others, domestic sovereign bonds, international bonds, investment-grade corporate securities, high-yield securities and inflation-protected bonds. Cash is represented by money market instruments.

Underlying funds can involve active management, which has led to the distinction between "active" and "passive" target date funds, depending on the type of products the fund is mostly invested in. While "active" funds attracted most of inflows until the end of the 2000's, passive funds have taken over since then and in its *2018 Target-Date Fund Landscape*, Morningstar estimated that only funds with "below average" or "low" fees had positive net flows in 2017 in the United States. Overall, "passive" funds attracted almost 95% of the $70 billion net flows in this year.[27] This trend has been pushed by an increasing concern over the level and the transparency of fees, which has affected the asset management industry.

It should be noted, yet, that the distinction between "active" and "passive" products is blurred by the use of index funds in so-called active funds. Moreover, the management rules of virtually all balanced funds and target date funds leave room for the managers to deviate from the neutral allocation stated in the convention in order to exploit investment opportunities that they deem favorable. In fact, discretion is left to the fund's provider in deciding which asset allocation is suitable for each investor's profile. This results in substantial variability in the glidepath across target date funds, as can be seen from Figure 14. Twenty years before the target date, the equity allocation ranges from 53% to 91%, and ten years after, it is comprised between 20% and 58%. Incidentally, the figure also highlights the aforementioned difference between "to" funds, in which the equity allocation lands on its minimum before or at the target date, and "through" funds, in which the landing occurs after the target is reached.

Target date funds are a widespread investment product in the United States. According to Morningstar (2018), net assets grew from $158 billion at the end of 2008 to $1.11 trillion at the end of 2017, with positive net inflows every year. An important explanation of this success is the status of a "Qualified Default

---

[27] Source: Morningstar (2018), Exhibits 3 and 5.

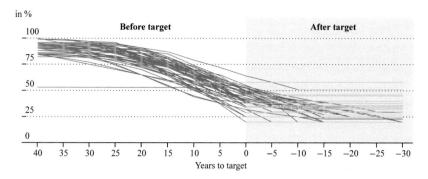

Figure 14 Equity glidepath of 58 US target date funds.
Notes: Data for the 58 US target date funds is borrowed from Appendix 2 of
Morningstar (2018), and it is as of December 31, 2017. The blue part of each line
represents the glidepath up to the landing point, defined as the date after which the
equity allocation no longer decreases, and the yellow part is the glidepath after the
landing point.

Investment Alternative" that these funds (and balanced funds) gained after the
Pension Protection Act that was passed in September 2006:[28] a QDIA is a fund
in which assets can be invested by the fiduciary of a pension plan, like a 401(k)
plan, unless the participant expresses a different wish.

5.2 How Consistent Is Advice with Modern Portfolio Theory?

The problem of planning consumption and investment has been the focus of a
large body of academic research since the seminal work by Paul A. Samuelson
and Robert C. Merton between 1969 and 1973, who introduced the mathematical framework to solve such optimization problems. Thus, a natural question
is whether conventional advice is consistent with the prescriptions of portfolio theory and to what extent balanced funds and target date funds proxy for
optimal portfolios.

One way to cast the problem of managing savings through accumulation
into this approach is to consider an agent who maximizes expected utility with
a horizon equal to the time to retirement. The solution is a function of various investor-specific parameters, like the horizon and the attitude toward risk,
and objective parameters, like the values of interest rates, expected returns and
volatilities. Three modeling assumptions have a key impact on the form of the
solution:

---

[28] See www.dol.gov/agencies/ebsa/about-ebsa/our-activities/resource-center/fact-sheets/default-
investment-alternatives-under-participant-directed-individual-account-plans.

- whether the agent derives utility from the nominal value of savings or from another quantity;
- whether investment opportunities, described by the expected returns, the volatilities and the correlations of portfolio constituents, are constant or vary stochastically over time; and
- whether the agent makes contributions to his/her savings account after the date at which the investment plan is set up.

The provided assumptions determine the *building blocks* that the agent should combine to form the optimal portfolio and the fraction of wealth that is optimally allocated to the building blocks. By playing with them, one arrives at different lists of building blocks and different allocation schemes. To rationalize conventional advice and existing accumulation products, a model must predict that more risk-averse investors should place a higher fraction of their savings in bonds than in stocks, and that young investors should hold a larger fraction of equities and should gradually switch to bonds as they age. But in a nutshell, it is hard to reconcile these recommendations with those of the models, for three main reasons:

- Models express optimal strategies through *fund separation theorems*, which state that the optimal portfolio is a combination of elementary portfolios invested in risky assets (i.e. stocks, bonds and alternative assets), and this separation in building blocks does not recoup the separation in asset classes that is adopted by mutual funds.
- The effects of risk aversion and investment horizon are much more complicated than those assumed in conventional advice. In particular, models do not predict that more risk-averse investors should place a larger fraction of their savings in less volatile asset classes.
- The optimal portfolio strategy depends on a number of *state variables* that characterize the opportunity set, including notably risk premia and volatilities, so that the portfolio composition is not a function of age alone but also of market conditions.

We now turn to examine these reasons in detail.

5.2.1 Optimal Building Blocks

In the simplest case, the agent has utility from terminal wealth, there is a single risky asset with constant expected return and volatility, and the agent makes no contributions after the initial one. Then, Merton (1971) shows that for a class of utility functions known as *hyperbolic absolute risk aversion*, the optimal portfolio combines the risky asset with the cash account.[29] In particular, when the "relative risk aversion coefficient" is constant,[30] the proportion of wealth invested in the risky asset is equal to the Sharpe ratio of the asset divided by its volatility, times the reciprocal of the relative risk aversion coefficient.[31] So, when relative risk aversion is constant, the optimal portfolio is a fixed mix. With multiple risky assets, like stocks and long-term bonds, the two building blocks of the solution are the *maximum Sharpe ratio portfolio* of the assets and the cash account.[32]

The optimal investment strategy gets much more complicated when investment opportunities vary over time, an assumption that is, of course, more realistic because the assumption of constant expected returns and volatilities implies that asset returns are independent and identically distributed over time, so that prices follow random walks. This restriction is at variance with a number of stylized facts about returns: stock and bond returns are predictable to a limited extent (e.g. with the dividend yield for stocks and the slope of the yield curve for bonds to mention but a few predictors), and the examination of historical stock returns suggests that periods of high volatility have alternated with periods of rest.

In this situation, Merton (1973) shows that the optimal portfolio involves new building blocks, in addition to the maximum Sharpe ratio portfolio of the risky assets and the cash account. Each of these elementary portfolios, which are called "funds" in Merton's article with reference to *fund separation theorems*, is intended to help the agent hedge against unexpected and unfavorable changes in the opportunity set.[33] For instance, if interest rates fall down, opportunities look worse, which adversely impacts investor's welfare. To hedge

---

[29] A hyperbolic absolute risk aversion utility function has the form

$$u(c) = \frac{1}{1-\gamma}\left[\frac{\beta c}{\gamma} + \eta\right]^{1-\gamma},$$

where β, γ and η are three constant parameters.

[30] Relative risk aversion is defined as $-cu''(c)/u'(c)$. The constant relative risk aversion utility function is obtained by letting $\eta = 0$ and $\beta = \gamma^{\gamma/[\gamma-1]}$ in the definition of a hyperbolic risk aversion function, so that the utility function is given by

$$u(c) = \frac{c^{1-\gamma}}{1-\gamma}.$$

[31] See Equation (40), p. 390, of Merton (1971).

[32] See Equation (16), p. 876, of Merton (1973).

[33] See Merton (1973), Theorem 2, p. 880–81. In the original article, Merton considers a single state variable to describe the opportunity set, so that the optimal portfolio is a combination of three building blocks. Merton (1992), Section 15.10, analyzes the general case, with multiple state variables.

against this event, an agent has to purchase assets that grow in value when rates decrease – that is, essentially, long-term bonds. Thus, a third building block appears, which is mainly made of long-term bonds.

To further complicate things, building blocks depend on the agent's objective. In the basic version of the Merton model, utility is derived from the nominal value of savings, but one can think of many situations in which this quantity is not the most appropriate. For instance, the purchasing power wealth in terms of goods and services may be a more relevant metrics for investors who plan to spend their savings on such items. Here, utility is derived from *real* wealth, which is wealth divided by the consumer price index. The introduction of inflation uncertainty brings a new building block, namely the inflation-hedging portfolio, because agents must invest at least part of their assets in a portfolio that hedges them against the risk of unexpected inflation shocks.[34] Similarly, a case can be made that in the context of retirement preparation, the nominal value of savings matters less than the amount of replacement income that these savings can finance. So, a better measure of welfare than the expected utility from wealth at retirement would be the expected utility from wealth divided by the retirement bond price. With this change in the agent's objective, the retirement bond will itself appear as a building block in the optimal strategy.[35]

To conclude, optimal portfolios are, in theory, made of multiple elementary "funds" that have functional definitions. The maximum Sharpe ratio portfolio delivers the best Sharpe ratio in the short run, the cash account cancels any uncertainty over short-term returns, and hedging portfolios are used to hedge against unfavorable changes in the opportunity set, including notably changes in interest rates and risk premia. This separation principle contrasts with the breakdown of standard mutual funds, which is generally expressed in terms of asset classes like domestic stocks, foreign stocks, Government bonds, investment-grade bonds and so on.

5.2.2 Effect of Risk Aversion

When investment opportunities are constant and the agent has constant relative risk aversion, the optimal strategy is to hold a fixed-mix portfolio of the risky assets and the cash account. This rule is reminiscent of the investment policy

---

[34] See Brennan and Xia (2002).

[35] See Proposition 2 in Martellini and Milhau (2012) for a related example in asset-liability management for a pension fund: if a pension fund has utility from its funding ratio, defined as assets divided by liabilities, the utility-maximizing strategy involves a long position in the liability-hedging portfolio, defined as the portfolio that replicates the value of liabilities. In retirement investing, the value of liabilities is replaced by the retirement bond price, and the retirement bond plays the role of the liability-hedging portfolio.

of balanced funds, but in contrast with conventional advice, it implies that risk aversion has no effect on the relative weighting of stocks and bonds. Stocks and bonds are weighted according to their risk and return characteristics, but a more risk-averse investor should not increase his/her allocation to bonds. He/she will only invest a greater percentage of wealth in the cash account versus the risky building block. Moreover, there is no horizon effect, as the optimal portfolio is a function of short-term risk and return parameters and the risk aversion level. To introduce horizon effects, the assumptions have to be altered, as explained below.

In the presence of stochastic investment opportunities, it is remarkable that the composition of the hedging portfolios is independent from the risk aversion (and also from the horizon), as established by Merton (1973), but the percentage allocation to each fund does. The dependence can be complex, as appears from the examples given in Kim and Omberg (1996) and Liu (2007). However, Wachter (2003) proves a general result, which holds regardless of the particular choice of a utility function, and regardless of the way investment opportunities are modeled: as risk aversion grows to infinity, agents should optimally hold the pure discount bond with residual maturity equal to their investment horizon. This result makes intuitive sense because infinitely risk averse investors are concerned only with the variance of their wealth at retirement, and the pure discount bond is the asset that yields a certain payoff. But importantly, this bond building block is not a generic bond portfolio, since it must replicate the returns on the pure discount bond. As a consequence, it must have the same duration – a duration that shrinks to zero as retirement approaches.

5.2.3 Rationalizing Horizon Effects with Stochastic Investment Opportunities

Horizon effects can arise when investment opportunities change stochastically over time. For instance, and as explained previously, models predict that investors with infinite risk aversion should invest in the pure discount bond with residual maturity equal to their horizon. This result, which is mathematically established by Wachter (2003), is consistent with the "preferred habitat" hypothesis of Modigliani and Sutch (1966), which postulates that investors are concerned with the interest rates of the maturities that correspond to their respective horizons. When interest rates vary over time, bonds of different maturities are not perfect substitutes for each other: the price at the retirement date of a bond that matures beyond this date is ex ante uncertain, and a bond that matures before retirement has to be reinvested in another bond, at a rate that is not known beforehand.

Another horizon effect is present if there is a single risky asset, interpreted as a stock index, and the risk premium over the risk-free rate varies over the business cycle, by increasing after a drop in prices and decreasing after a rise. This case is solved analytically by Kim and Omberg (1996), and the optimal stock-cash allocation depends on the horizon because the agent can invest in the stock for strategic purposes. Indeed, the stock serves as a hedge against a deterioration in investment opportunities because it tends to display high returns at times its expected return is low. Thus, by investing in stocks, the agent can hedge against the risk of negative shocks on welfare caused by drops in the stock risk premium. This effect is more present for long investment horizons, so the *hedging demand* for stocks tends to increase with the horizon. But the optimal stock-cash allocation depends on the current value of the risk premium, so it is not a deterministic function of time, and it differs from the deterministic glidepath of target date funds.

5.2.4 Role of Nonfinancial Income

Horizon effects also arise if contributions take place during the accumulation period. Indeed, Merton (1969) shows that if an investor receives "nonfinancial income," defined as income from nonportfolio sources, like labor earnings, the optimal dollar allocation to each risky asset is the same as the optimal dollar allocation for an otherwise identical investor who would receive no income from outside the portfolio but would be endowed with the sum of financial wealth plus the discounted value of future income inflows. To express this rule mathematically, consider the case where the investor receives constant income, has constant relative risk aversion γ, faces constant investment opportunities and has access to both a single risky asset with Sharpe ratio λ and volatility σ, and a cash account. Let H denote the value of the *human capital*, which is the present value of future income inflows discounted at the risk-free interest rate, and W be the value of financial wealth. Then, *total wealth* is $W + H$. If there were no nonportfolio income, the optimal percentage allocation to the risky asset would be $\lambda/[\gamma\sigma^2]$, according to Merton's optimality theorem.[36] Merton shows that if w is the optimal percentage allocation for the agent endowed with income, we have[37]

$$wW = \frac{\lambda}{\gamma\sigma^2}[W + H],$$

---

[36] See Equation (49) in Merton (1969).
[37] See Equation (71) in Merton (1969).

so that

$$w = \frac{\lambda}{\gamma \sigma^2} \left[1 + \frac{H}{W} \right].$$

The rest of financial wealth, corresponding to the percentage $1 - w$, is invested in cash.

The presence of nonportfolio income introduces a horizon effect, because the ratio H/W tends to be larger for younger individuals: indeed, these have usually little financial wealth and a large human capital, while individuals near retirement have accumulated capital but have less forthcoming income. If the risky asset is interpreted as a stock index, this result indeed implies that investors should progressively replace stocks with bonds as they get older. But this substitution does not take place at a deterministic rate, since it is driven by the ratio H/W, which depends on how wealth grows and thus depends on the returns on the risky asset.

But constant investment opportunities and constant income are a rather crude model. Models with uncertain income and/or opportunities are more difficult to solve, although the general idea is the same: an investor with constant relative risk aversion should have the same dollar allocation to risky assets as an otherwise identical investor with no nonportfolio income but a greater total wealth, and he/she should take a short position in the portfolio that replicates the returns on the human capital. By this criterion, employees should not own stocks of their own company because this would overexpose them to company's risk, so that salaries would be cut and savings would melt if it went through bad times. But whether such models rationalize gradual substitution of bonds for stocks crucially depends on how income is modeled, as Benzoni, Collin-Dufresne and Goldstein (2007) have shown. If income is treated as deterministic, the human capital is bond-like, so that young individuals should hold more stocks than their elders, but if income is linked to stock dividends, the human capital is stock-like and the optimal stock allocation is a hump-shaped function of age. Then, it is not necessarily optimal for younger individuals to invest more in stocks.

5.3 Better Building Blocks

5.3.1 Problems with the Traditional "Safe" Building Block

As they approach their target date, target date funds shift toward a "safe" building block invested in bonds and cash, with the purpose of reducing the risk of losses with respect to a stock investment and also, for "through" funds, the purpose of generating income in retirement. But for this portfolio to be truly safe for the wealth accumulation objective, it should have a certain rate of return between the current date and the retirement date. In other words, it should replicate the returns of a pure discount bond maturing at this date, so that an investor solely concerned with the dispersion of the value of his/her savings at retirement would be able to eliminate any uncertainty by investing in it. To do so, the duration of the bond bucket should vanish as the retirement date approaches. If it does not, residual interest rate risk exposure subsists, and even if he/she is entirely invested in the "safe" portfolio, an individual is still exposed to the risk of capital losses in case interest rates increase. This property is at odds with the stated objective to reduce the risk of losses near retirement.

So, a first way to improve target date funds would be to recognize that not only the allocation to the "risky" and the "safe" building blocks should depend on the horizon, but the composition of the "safe" bucket cannot be identical for all horizons: the "safe" building block for a T-year horizon should replicate the returns of a T-year pure discount bond, so it should have a duration equal to that of this bond. As a consequence, it cannot be the same for a 20-year and for a 5-year horizon, and this problem cannot be addressed by adjusting the glidepath. Constructing a truly safe portfolio requires a proper allocation to bonds and cash so as to reach target exposures to interest rate risk factors, including notably a target duration.

But, the nominal value of savings is less relevant for future retirees than the amount of replacement income that they can purchase with these savings. This has important consequences for the definition of the risk-free asset, because a pure discount bond is not risk-free for the income-generation objective, even if it matures at the retirement date. Indeed, each dollar invested in the bond during the accumulation phase gives $\$1 + r$ when the individual retires, where r is the simple return on the bond between the contribution date and the retirement date. This return is known at the time the contribution is made. But the individual discovers how much income the $\$1 + r$ can purchase only when he/she retires, because the retirement bond price is not known in advance. The problem is that while the *absolute* return of the pure discount bond is known at the time a contribution is made, its *relative* return with respect to the retirement bond is not.

Again, this problem is not solved by changing the equity glidepath of the target date fund, and it calls for the use of a "safe" building block that is consistent with the objective. Since the end goal is to generate replacement income in retirement, the proper "safe" asset is the retirement bond itself. If this bond is not readily available in financial markets, the safe asset is a portfolio of traded securities that replicates its returns.

5.3.2 Performance-Seeking Portfolio

In balanced funds and target date funds, equities are intended to bring greater long-term returns than bonds and cash, so as to boost savings for investors with a long horizon. Adopting a goal-based approach of the accumulation problem leads to slightly rephrase this role. As explained in Section 5.4, what matters in goal-based investing for retirement is the relative return of a portfolio strategy with respect to the retirement bond, and the strategy helps investors reach income levels that they are unable to secure with their current resources alone if it outperforms the retirement bond. So, the intended function of equities in goal-based investing strategies is to outperform the retirement bond in the long run.

Equities are the only asset class suitable for that purpose, and alternative asset classes can also be used as long as liquid and cost-efficient vehicles exist to invest in them. For this reason, we coin the term "performance-seeking portfolio," which is more general than "equities" and highlights the role of the portfolio, which is to generate performance above and beyond the retirement bond, rather than a particular asset class. This name change is consistent with the prescriptions of fund separation theorems in asset-liability management,[38] which describe welfare-maximizing investment policies as combinations of two building blocks: a liability-hedging portfolio, which is the institutional equivalent for the retirement bond, and a performance-seeking portfolio, which should be in theory the maximum Sharpe ratio portfolio of available risky assets. Thus, separation is not expressed in terms of asset classes like stocks and bonds, but in terms of functional building blocks that have well-defined roles.

If the performance-seeking portfolio (henceforth, PSP) is invested in equities, many funds are available, ranging from active funds to passive funds that replicate the performance of indices. Because active management often fails to deliver better returns than its benchmarks after adjusting for fees, the authors' position is to favor passive products. Exchange-traded funds (ETFs) provide cheap and easy access to the risk premia that exist in equity markets, which makes them particularly suitable for strategies requiring rebalancing.[39]

Also, it should be noted that not all equity indices have equally attractive risk-return profiles. It is now widely recognized that cap-weighted indices, which have long been the default choice for the benchmarking of equity portfolios, are far from offering the best possible risk-return tradeoff. To illustrate this point, Table 2 displays the annualized return, the volatility and the Sharpe

---

[38] See Amenc et al. (2010) for examples of fund separation theorems.
[39] See Amenc, Goltz and Grigoriu (2010) for examples of dynamic trading strategies using ETFs as building blocks.

Table 2 Performance and risk indicators for US cap-weighted or smart beta equity indices, June 1970 to December 2016.

Universe	Weighting	Annualized return (%)	Annualized volatility (%)	Sharpe ratio
All	Cap-weighted	10.59	16.74	0.33
	Equally weighted	12.18	16.56	0.43
	Minimum variance	12.58	14.23	0.53
	Maximum Sharpe ratio	12.59	15.44	0.49
Mid cap	Cap-weighted	12.50	17.03	0.44
	Equally weighted	12.96	16.78	0.48
	Minimum variance	13.61	14.05	0.61
	Maximum Sharpe ratio	13.37	15.53	0.54
Value	Cap-weighted	11.60	16.71	0.40
	Equally weighted	13.34	16.30	0.51
	Minimum variance	13.59	14.17	0.61
	Maximum Sharpe ratio	13.89	15.37	0.58
High momentum	Cap-weighted	11.45	17.13	0.38
	Equally weighted	12.75	16.96	0.46
	Minimum variance	13.86	14.88	0.60
	Maximum Sharpe ratio	13.26	16.04	0.52
Low volatility	Cap-weighted	10.86	14.99	0.39
	Equally weighted	12.71	13.69	0.56
	Minimum variance	13.01	12.69	0.63
	Maximum Sharpe ratio	13.06	13.16	0.61
Low investment	Cap-weighted	11.90	15.58	0.44
	Equally weighted	13.47	15.20	0.56
	Minimum variance	14.08	13.49	0.67
	Maximum Sharpe ratio	13.90	14.50	0.61

(Continued)

High	Cap-weighted	11.03	16.99	0.36
profitability	Equally weighted	12.69	17.04	0.45
	Minimum variance	13.02	14.56	0.55
	Maximum Sharpe ratio	13.14	15.78	0.52

Notes: Equity indices are constructed from US stocks. Universe "All" contains the 500 largest stocks, and the other universes are made of the 250 stocks with the smallest capitalization, the lowest investment (past 2-year asset growth), the highest momentum score (return over past 52 weeks minus most recent 4 weeks), the highest gross profitability (gross profit divided by total assets), the lowest past 2-year volatility or the highest book-to-market ratio. Cap-weighted indices are weighted by market capitalization, minimum variance indices are weighted so as to minimize the ex ante portfolio variance, and maximum Sharpe ratio indices are designed to maximize the ex ante Sharpe ratio. Non-negativity constraints are applied to rule out short positions, and liquidity and turnover adjustments are done in order to ensure investability of all indices. Data is from the long-term track records of the Scientific Beta database. The start date is June 19, 1970, and the end date is December 21, 2016. Details on the universe construction and the index calculation can be found in Scientific Beta (2018, 2019). In maximum Sharpe ratio indices, expected returns are assumed to be proportional to the semi-standard deviations of stocks.

ratio of a range of US equity indices calculated by Scientific Beta over a 46.5-year period that starts in June 1970 and ends in December 2016. The broad cap-weighted index has the lowest annualized return (10.59%) and the lowest Sharpe ratio (0.33) across the 28 indices, and in each sub-universe, made of half the stocks contained in the broad universe, it is also the cap-weighted portfolio that features both the lowest performance and the lowest Sharpe ratio.

Each sub-universe is defined by a stock selection that exposes the portfolio to an equity factor known for being rewarded in the long run. Four decades of research on the sources of risk premia in equities, from the early 1970s to 2016, have led to the publication of over 300 factors, according to the survey of Harvey, Liu and Zhu (2016), but only a handful have stood repeated tests for statistical robustness and are economically justified. Table 2 retains six factors for which research has documented a risk premium that is persistent over time and across geographic zones, and for which economic justification exists:[40]

---

[40] See Amenc et al. (2015) for a survey of empirical evidence in favor of the risk premia and the economic justifications. Risk-based explanations for premia state that a factor is rewarded because it correlates with the marginal utility of consumption, so that a security more exposed to that factor displays higher returns when marginal utility is low – that is, when such high returns are less needed (see Martellini and Milhau 2015). Behavioral explanations contend that observed risk premia result from systematic mistakes made by the market in valuing securities,

size, value, momentum, volatility, investment and profitability. As explained by Amenc et al. (2014b), cap-weighted indices suffer from two shortcomings. First, they do not provide investors with exposures to rewarded risk factors, and they are even negatively exposed to some of these factors, like size. Second, weighting by capitalization implies heavy concentration in a few very large stocks, so that these indices are not much diversified and they involve a substantial amount of unrewarded, or stock-specific, risks. "Smart factor" equity indices aim to address these problems by providing exposures to rewarded risk factors and by diversifying away as much as possible of unrewarded risks. The second step of their construction, or "smart weighting," consists in weighting stocks equally or in weighting them according to their volatilities and correlations.

The empirical evidence summarized in Table 2 shows that both deviations from broad cap-weighted indexation help improve average returns and the Sharpe ratios, since the cap-weighted index of each universe dominates the broad cap-weighted index with respect to both criteria, and the non-cap-weighted indices bring further improvement. All this suggests that smart factor indices have greater probabilities to outperform the retirement bond than a standard broad cap-weighted index has and that, as such, they would be more attractive in accumulation investment strategies. As a last comment, let us mention that different equity indices can also be combined together, so as to capture several risk premia and to benefit from staggered performance cycles of the various factors. Amenc et al. (2014a) give examples of multifactor allocations.

5.3.3 Mass-Customization of Funds

The modified balanced funds and target date funds that we describe in this section are invested in a PSP and a retirement bond. Because the retirement bond is for a specific retirement date, for a given decumulation period and for a given annual cost-of-living adjustment (COLA), each fund inherits these characteristics. The duration of the decumulation period can be taken equal to the rounded life expectancy at retirement. Assuming that most individuals retire around 65, this implies a duration of 20 years. As far as the COLA is concerned, one can take an estimate for long-term expected inflation, say 2% in the European Monetary Union and in the United States, since it is the long-term target of the central banks in these areas (see Section 4.1). These values are generic and not necessarily representative of the situation of a particular individual, and it would be possible in principle to use customized values, but the funds thus

owing to investor's behavioral biases, and that these mistakes cannot be arbitraged away due to the existence of limits to arbitrage.

constructed would be tailored products, which would not be suitable for other individuals. The idea is instead to design *mass-customized* funds, which can accommodate the needs of a large class of investors.

Unlike the life expectancy and the expected inflation, the retirement date varies greatly and in an observable way across individuals, so even imperfectly customized products must offer different choices. Such is already the practice for target date funds, and individuals are invited to join the fund with the nearest target date to their expected retirement date. The same system would be implemented for funds using the retirement bond as a safe building block.

5.4 Goal-Based Investing for Retirement

5.4.1 Absolute Wealth versus Relative Wealth

With the income-generation goal in mind, the quantity of interest should not be the nominal value of savings, but instead their purchasing power in terms of replacement income, which equals savings divided by the price of one dollar of replacement income in retirement – that is, the retirement bond price. Equation (4.4) is the formal expression of this definition. Moving the focus from nominal wealth to the purchasing power of wealth brings a significant change with respect to current practices, but it is a key step in the setup of a *goal-based investing* approach. Indeed, what matters in goal-based investing is not how much savings are accumulated, but whether or not savings are sufficient to reach a goal and how much more money is needed to be successful in case the target is not yet met.

The change in focus from absolute to relative wealth also has implications for how the returns of a portfolio should be measured during accumulation. As shown in Equation (4.7), the change in the purchasing power of savings between two dates equals the relative return of the savings account with respect to the retirement bond between these dates, so the relative return matters less than the absolute one. Thus, the natural benchmark for accumulation strategies is the retirement bond. But beating this benchmark is not the end goal; it is useful because it serves the goal of increasing the amount of income that an investor can finance with his/her savings. In other words, it is useful to the extent that it helps individuals to reach "aspirational goals," as defined in Section 4.3.

5.4.2 Funding Status of Goals

By checking the affordable income level, an individual can assess his/her situation relative to a goal, defined as a level of replacement income (see

Section 4.3). Suppose that he/she has a target income level in mind and consider a date in the accumulation period. If the affordable income level at that date is greater than the target, the goal is said to be *affordable* or *reached*: in other words, the individual has accumulated enough money to secure it and does not need to make new savings. But as explained shortly, he/she still has to make appropriate investment choices to make sure that the goal is effectively secured, because not any portfolio strategy will preserve the affordable status of the goal until retirement.

If the affordable income level is less than the target, the goal is not affordable, and according to the definitions given in Section 4.3, it is an *aspirational* goal. By definition, an aspirational goal cannot be reached with certainty by the retirement date, but the individual can undertake two actions to give himself/herself a chance of success: save more by making new contributions, and choose a portfolio strategy that has the potential to outperform the retirement bond. The success probability, which is the probability of reaching an aspirational goal, can be estimated by running Monte-Carlo simulations of future savings values and future prices of the retirement bond. These simulations rely on assumptions on the values of future contributions and on the future returns of the fund(s) in which they are invested. Examples are given in Section 5.5 below. That way, the individual can get a sense of how likely it is for the goal to be reached by the retirement date.

5.4.3 Stop-Gain Decisions

If a goal, defined as a target level of replacement income, is affordable at some point in the accumulation phase, the individual has essentially to decide whether he/she is satisfied with this level or if he/she wants to go beyond it. In the former case, no additional contributions are needed, so the individual can stop saving for retirement, but he/she has to make sure that the goal stays affordable until he/she retires. To secure a reached goal, he/she must transfer his/her retirement assets to the retirement bond, because it is the only asset that preserves the purchasing power of savings in terms of replacement income across all market conditions. As explained in Section 4.4, assets usually regarded as safe, like bonds and cash, are unable to offer the same guarantee except by chance, so they do not offer a reliable protection. The action of transferring savings from the portfolio in which they are invested to the retirement bond is a *stop-gain decision*.

The possibility for individuals to make stop-gain decisions has important implications for the estimation of the probabilities of reaching aspirational goals. Indeed, these probabilities are calculated by simulating the future returns on a portfolio strategy (including future contributions) and those on the retirement bond that corresponds to the individual's profile, and to each simulated scenario, a 0-1 score is assigned depending on whether the goal is reached or not: 0 means failure and 1 means success. But if an individual has the option, at any time, to switch to the retirement bond to secure the purchasing power of his/her savings, the score 1 should be given to any scenario in which the purchasing power becomes greater than or equal to the target *at least once* during the accumulation phase. If the possibility of stop-gain decisions during accumulation did not exist, score 1 would be reserved for scenarios in which the purchasing power *at* retirement date is greater than or equal to the target. Clearly, taking into account the opportunity of stop-gain decisions leads to higher success probabilities than ignoring it: by forgoing this possibility, individuals would miss chances to secure a reached goal.

Of course, a stop-gain can only be done if the retirement bond is part of the investment universe during accumulation, or at least if it can be synthesized with available assets. In the absence of this bond and of a replicating strategy during the accumulation phase, an investor is unable to secure a given stream of replacement income until he/she retires.

The other decision that an individual can make if the target income level is affordable is to revise his/her goal and to target an even higher level. By definition, this new goal is aspirational, so that the individual is back to the decision to contribute more and/or to choose an investment strategy that can potentially outperform the retirement bond. But he/she may also not want to start from scratch, and may be willing to preserve some of the purchasing power of already accumulated savings. If he/she wants to protect 100% of the purchasing power, he/she has to make a stop-gain decision and to transfer existing savings to the retirement bond, but a full switch to this asset is not needed if he/she wants to protect some fraction, say 90%, 80% or any other percentage. In the goal-based investing framework introduced by Chhabra (2005) and subsequently formalized by Deguest et al. (2015), an affordable goal that the investor wants to secure is an *essential goal*. So, the task is to set up a savings and investment plan that secures the essential goal while maintaining room for the achievement of aspirational goals.

This task is by no means trivial, and it cannot be accomplished by individual investors who do not have a strong financial background without external and professional advice, whether it comes from a traditional human advisor or, more likely for individuals who cannot afford customized advice, from a robo-advisor. Indeed, there are many strategies that can secure an essential goal, but they are not equal in terms of upside potential, and they can be more or less reliable as far as the protection of the goal is concerned.

Section 6 describes a set of such strategies and discusses their merits and their drawbacks.

5.5 Benefits for Individuals

We now simulate the returns of "standard" balanced and target date funds invested in a cap-weighted US equity index and a Treasury index, and their "modified" versions, in which the bond building block is taken to be the retirement bond. The objective is to examine the respective evolutions of savings and of the affordable income level over time under the various investment strategies and to see how the change in the building block affects the risk and return properties of a given investment rule.

5.5.1 Comparing Strategies in Goal-Based Investing

It is standard in asset management to report average returns and volatilities in absolute terms, but as argued in Section 5.4, *relative* risk and return metrics are more appropriate in a goal-based framework because an investor is more concerned with the amount of income that he/she can finance than with the nominal value of savings. Beyond the distinction between absolute and relative indicators, risk is also a polysemic notion: it can refer to uncertainty over wealth or over the purchasing power of wealth in terms of income, or to the risk of a loss in either of these quantities. In the former sense, risk is usually measured as volatility, whose limitation as a risk measure is that it treats downside and upside deviations from the mean equally. This shortcoming is addressed by downside risk measures such as the annual loss, the semivolatility or the maximum drawdown. We focus on annual losses, which are an easily interpretable indicator for individuals.

To simulate the returns of mutual funds, we need constituents' returns, and for the purpose of checking the evolution of the purchasing power of savings, we also need the returns on the retirement bond. We first present a backtest conducted with historical equity and interest rate data, because such a backtest gives a sense of how the strategies would have behaved if they had been implemented in the past, up to the inclusion of transaction costs and taxes, and it helps to convey some important properties of the various strategies. But backtests are not sufficient to compare goal-based investing strategies: a strategy should not be preferred over another because it has a better track record, but because it has an ex ante better ability to reach an individual's goals. Thus, we also compare the strategies by using a Monte-Carlo model for the simulation of multiple scenarios for constituents' returns and interest rates.

5.5.2 Historical Backtest

We consider an individual who retires on January 1, 2019, and has the choice between four mutual funds that follow different investment strategies:

- a "standard" balanced fund (abbreviated as "standard BF") with 40% in US equities and 60% in a Treasury bond index;
- a "modified" balanced fund with the same percentage in equities, and the rest in the retirement bond for an individual who accumulates until January 2019;
- a "standard" target date fund (in short, "standard TDF") that begins with 60% in equities 20 years before retirement, in January 1999, and ends with 20% the year before retirement (the rest of the fund is invested in the Treasury bond index); or
- a "modified" target date fund with the same equity glidepath as the standard TDF but a different bond portfolio since the Treasury index is replaced with the retirement bond.

The equity glidepath of the two target date funds is depicted in Figure 15. All four funds are rebalanced every quarter to their target allocation.

Figure 16 shows the simulated value of $100,000 invested in each of the four funds, and the purchasing power of the pension pot in terms of income. This backtest comes with its inherent limitations: transaction costs and taxes are not included here and the funds are fictitious, especially for those that invest in the retirement bond, which did not exist in the past. Besides, for the period from January 1999 to December 2007, some of the cash flows of the retirement bond

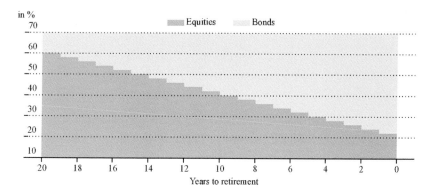

Figure 15 Example of equity glidepath for target date funds.
Notes: In the standard target date fund, the bond building block is a broad US Treasury index, and in the modified fund, it is the retirement bond for an individual who retires at the fund target date.

(a) Value of savings.

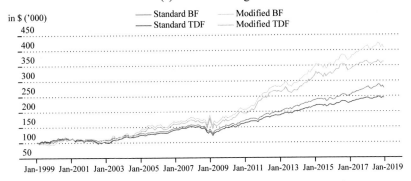

(b) Purchasing power of savings in terms of replacement income.

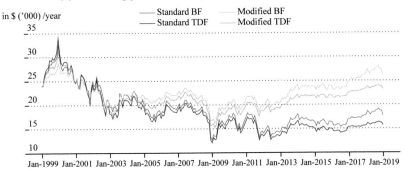

Figure 16 Evolution of $100,000 invested on January 1, 1999, in mutual funds, from 1999 to 2019.

Notes: Panel (a) shows the value of $100,000 invested on January 1, 1999, in two balanced funds (BF) and two target date funds (TDF). The standard funds are invested in an equity index (the S&P 500 index with dividends reinvested) and in a Treasury bond index (the Barclays US Treasury index), and the modified funds are invested in the same equity portfolio and in the retirement bond for an individual who retires in 2019. The retirement bond is priced by discounting future cash flows with US sovereign zero-coupon rates. Panel (b) displays the amount of income that can be financed with savings at each point in time. Income cash flows (without a COLA) begin in January 2019 and occur every year until January 2038.

have a maturity longer than 30 years, since the last cash flow occurs in January 2038. Because the maximum maturity available in the US zero-coupon curve from the Federal Reserve website is 30 years (see Table 1), a discount rate is assigned to cash flows beyond this maturity by extrapolating the 30-year rate.

In this sample period, the retirement bond outperformed the bond index, which is why the modified funds outperformed their standard counterparts (see Table 3). This outperformance was due to the decrease in interest rates and the duration spread between the retirement bond and the index: indeed, the index duration was comprised between 5 and 7 years during this period, while that of

Table 3 Summary statistics on mutual funds and their constituents, from 1999 to 2019.

	Annual return (%)	Annual volatility (%)	Tracking error / ret. bond (%)	Maximum drawdown (%)	Maximum drawdown / ret. bond (%)
Standard BF	5.21	6.95	16.71	20.01	63.08
Modified BF	7.28	10.17	10.81	19.72	45.17
Standard TDF	4.57	7.85	17.30	21.50	66.27
Modified TDF	6.65	10.14	12.11	23.28	52.77
Equities	5.62	19.09	27.82	55.25	82.14
Bond index	4.15	4.50	11.71	7.17	54.54
Retirement bond	6.81	15.62	0.00	29.84	0.00

Notes: "BF" stands for "balanced fund" and "TDF" for "target date fund." The standard funds are invested in equities and the bond index, and the modified ones in equities and the retirement bond. All funds are rebalanced on a quarterly basis. Volatilities and tracking errors are estimated from daily returns. The maximum relative drawdown is the maximum drawdown of the time series of the purchasing power series, where the purchasing power (in terms of replacement income) is obtained by dividing savings by the retirement bond price.

the retirement bond was always greater, ranging from approximately 8.5 years at the end of accumulation to 27.8 years at the beginning. The longer duration of the retirement bond also accounts for its relatively large volatility, of 15.29%, and consequently for the fact that modified funds are more volatile than the standard ones. But, unsurprisingly, the substitution of the bond index with the retirement bond decreases relative risk, whether measured by the tracking error with respect to the retirement bond or with the maximum relative drawdown.

Another characteristic of the sample period is that equities underperformed the retirement bond, earning 5.62% per year on average, versus 6.81% for the bond. As a result, modified funds did not allow the individual to reach much higher levels of replacement income than what he/she could finance in 1999. Only the modified balanced fund lets the purchasing power of savings slightly grow: with $100,000, the individual could purchase $23,925 in 1999, and by

2019, savings had grown to $407,439, which was sufficient to purchase $26,124 per year. So, the modified balanced fund outperformed the bond, although both of its constituents underperformed this benchmark. This is a manifestation of the *rebalancing effect*, which causes a rebalanced portfolio to outperform its constituents in certain market conditions.[41]

By definition, any level of income greater than $23,925 per year is an *aspirational goal* in January 1999. By investing in the standard target date fund, the highest aspirational goal that the individual could reach between 1999 and 2019 was $33,997 per year, which is 142.1% of the initial level. But to secure it, he/she had to make a stop-gain decision by switching to the retirement bond when this level was reached, in January 2000. By staying in the fund until retirement, the level of income eventually reached was $15,660, which is only 65.5% of the initial level and 46.1% of the maximum over the period. More generally, for a given strategy, the aspirational goals reached over the period are those comprised between the initial level of income and the maximum over the period.

An inherent limitation of the analysis over a single scenario is that it does not allow the ex ante *probabilities* of reaching aspirational goals to be calculated. Strictly speaking, these probabilities can only be estimated as 100% or 0%, depending on whether the goal was reached or missed in that particular scenario, but success or failure can be an effect or good or bad luck, so that strategies cannot be compared to each other by this criterion. To estimate success probabilities, one needs to average multiple scenarios, as we explore in the following discussion.

5.5.3 Comparison via Stochastic Scenarios

To generate multiple scenarios, we use a stochastic continuous-time model for the risk factors involved in the analysis. The model is described formally in Appendix C.1, but its main characteristics are as follows. The value of the equity portfolio is modeled as a process with an annual volatility of 16.2% and an expected excess return over the risk-free interest rate of 6.4% per year. The nominal term structure is generated by the model of Vasicek (1977), and the model parameters are calibrated to the zero-coupon dataset from the Federal Reserve website of January 1, 2019. The bond index is modeled as a constant-maturity bond in the Vasicek model, with a maturity of 2 years: a constant-maturity bond is a continuous roll over of 2-year bonds. Its volatility is 1.38% per year, and its expected return over the risk-free rate is 0.30%

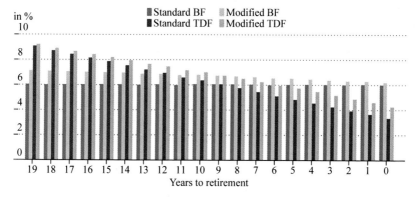

(a) Average annual volatility across scenarios.

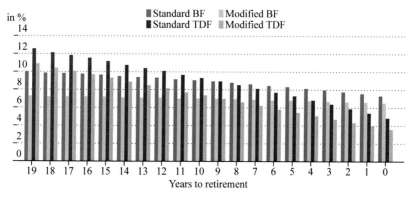

(b) Average tracking error with respect to retirement bond across scenarios.

Figure 17 Absolute and relative risk of mutual funds in stochastic scenarios, with January 2019 parameters.

Notes: The volatility and tracking error are first calculated from monthly returns in each scenario, and then averaged across the 10,000 scenarios. The tracking error is taken with respect to the retirement bond. Parameters of the interest rate model are fitted to the zero-coupon yield curve of the United States on January 1, 2019.

per year. With the assumed parameter values, the bond index, the stock index and the retirement bond earned, on average, 2.52%, 7.67% and 3.27% per year during the accumulation period, with annual volatilities of 1.39%, 16.16% and 6.86%.

Figure 17 displays the average volatilities and the average tracking errors with respect to the retirement bond of the four mutual funds in each year of the accumulation phase. The standard balanced fund has constant volatility over time, because it is a fixed-mix portfolio invested in two indices with stationary volatilities. On the other hand, the standard target date fund has decreasing volatility because it shifts away from equities (the more volatile asset) to bonds (the less volatile one), according to the glidepath shown in Figure 15. Both these funds have also decreasing tracking errors with respect to the retirement bond, because this bond has decreasing volatility over time: indeed, its volatility in the one-factor Vasicek model is proportional to its exposure to interest rate risk, and this exposure decreases as the maturities of the cash flows do so.

With each passing year, the modified funds have lower tracking errors than the standard ones, which implies that an individual faces less short-term uncertainty over replacement income with these funds. It is also seen that the relative risk profile of modified funds reflects the absolute risk profile of standard funds: the modified balanced fund has stable tracking error over time, but the relative risk of the modified target date fund decreases from 10.90% 19 years before retirement down to 3.59% in the last 12 months of accumulation.[42]

Table 4 summarizes the distribution of relative returns at retirement. These returns measure the change in the purchasing power of invested savings between the beginning and the end of accumulation, so that a return less than 100% means that the individual lost purchasing power, and a return greater than 100% means that he or she gained some. The replacement of the bond index with the retirement bond implies a reduction in the uncertainty over the final level of replacement income, whether measured by the standard deviation or by the spread between the minimum and the maximum of the distribution. The 75% success level, which is the relative return achieved with a 75% probability, is also higher with the modified funds than with the standard ones. This shows that the use of the truly safe building block in a portfolio not only implies lower uncertainty, but it also ensures that the strategy can keep up with its benchmark. In this simulation, the bond index has difficulties keeping up because it grows at 2.52% per year, versus 3.27% for the retirement bond, so the substitution ensures that the strategy does not underperform its benchmark too often.

Table 4 shows that although the distributions of relative returns with modified funds have lower maxima than those of standard funds, they have greater means and greater 75th percentiles. This suggests that modified funds do not have less upside potential relative to the retirement bond, except when it comes to reaching very ambitious goals. To further analyze this point, we now look at the aspirational goals attained by the various strategies. Recall that an aspirational goal is defined as a level of replacement income greater than the initial one. Since the parameters of the interest rate model are fitted to the US zero-coupon yield curve of January 1, 2019, the model-implied retirement bond price

---

[42] In fact, the tracking error of the modified balanced fund slightly decreases (from 7.28% to 6.52%), because the tracking error of the equity portfolio with respect to the retirement bond itself decreases, as a result of the diminishing volatility of the retirement bond.

Table 4 Dispersion of relative returns at retirement in stochastic scenarios, simulated with January 2019 parameters.

	Minimum (%)	25th percentile (%)	Mean (%)	75th percentile (%)	Maximum (%)	Standard deviation (%)
Standard BF	34.09	103.30	146.84	175.51	757.64	61.44
Modified BF	44.36	121.38	158.78	186.37	581.10	52.38
Standard TDF	31.67	103.21	148.63	179.62	790.94	65.05
Modified TDF	38.06	118.90	159.90	189.74	630.12	57.40

Notes: The relative return is the gross return of the mutual fund over the accumulation period, divided by the gross return of the retirement bond. Parameters of the interest rate model are fitted to the zero-coupon yield curve of the United States on January 1, 2019.

at the initial date is close to the price inferred from the actual yield curve. As a result, the initial level of replacement income, which is $12,116 per year, is close to the purchasing power of $100,000 on January 1, 2019, as implied by the zero-coupon yield curve on this date, which is $12,228 per year.

If the individual has the possibility to make stop-gain decisions – that is, if he/she has access to the retirement bond at any point in the accumulation period – an aspirational goal is reached within a period if, and only if, the purchasing power of savings is greater than or equal to this goal at least once during this period. Here, we are comparing standard mutual funds, invested in equities and a bond index, and modified funds, in which the bond index is replaced by the retirement bond. With the former investment option, it is in fact more consistent to assume that the retirement bond is not part of the investment universe, so that stop-gain decisions are impossible to make. Then, an aspirational goal is reached within a period only if the purchasing power of savings *at the end* of the period is greater than or equal to the goal. With this measurement approach, probabilities of reaching aspirational goals are mechanically lower than if a stop-gain decision can be implemented.

For these reasons, we consider both situations – with or without stop-gain decisions – in Figure 18. Panel (a) shows the level of replacement income attained with 75% probability at each point in the accumulation phase, still assuming that $100,000 are invested at the beginning, and assuming away the possibility of stop-gains. The exact mathematical definition of this indicator is the 25th percentile of the distribution of the income level at each point in time. In Panel (b), a different definition of success in reaching a goal is adopted, which assumes that stop-gains are possible. At each point in time, we calculate the highest income level that was attained with 75% probability between the beginning of accumulation and the current date. Technically, this quantity is the 25th percentile of the distribution of the maximum income level reached between the first date and the current date. By construction, it is increasing over time, for if a goal is reached during the first n years of accumulation, it is necessarily reached within the first $n + 1$ years.

Regardless of how the success probability is calculated, modified funds dominate their standard counterparts in that they allow higher levels of income to be reached with 75% probability. The spread is largest when stop-gains are not possible with standard funds, and when they are possible with modified funds. For instance, the level reached with 75% probability by the standard target date fund at the end of accumulation is $12,505 per year, which is hardly greater than the initial $12,116 per year. If the individual has access to the modified target date fund and can switch to the retirement bond at any point in accumulation, he/she can expect to reach not $12,505 but $16,098 per year. This corresponds

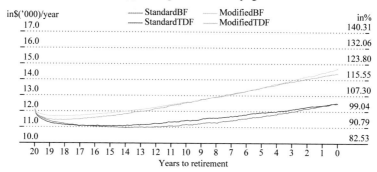

(a) Strategies without stop–gain.

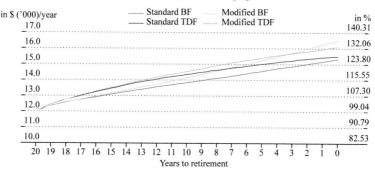

(b) Strategies with stop–gain.

Figure 18 Level of replacement income attained with 75% probability by investing $100,000 20 years before retirement, simulated with January 2019 parameters.

Notes: The left axis shows the level of replacement income in $('000) per year, and the right axis expresses this level as a percentage of the initial level, which is $12,116 per year. Tick marks of the right axis are rounded values, so the step between two consecutive values may not be strictly constant.

to a growth by 32.9% in the purchasing power of savings. In the intermediate, but somewhat contrived, case where the modified target date fund is not available but the retirement bond is, the income level reached with 75% probability is $15,496 per year, which is still less than with the modified fund. Similar observations can be repeated for balanced funds.

A comparison between the rightmost points for modified funds in Panels (a) and (b) also shows the strong impact of stop-gain decisions on success probabilities. If an individual is forced to stay in the fund until retirement, the modified balanced and target date funds reach $14,706 and $14,407 per year with 75% probability. But if a stop-gain decision can be made at any point in accumulation, the levels reached with 75% chances grow to $16,511 and $16,098 per year.

6 Applying Risk-Budgeting Techniques in Retirement Investing

The last part of this Element focuses on a specific class of investment strategies for accumulation known as *risk-controlled* strategies. Their broad objective is to secure a minimum level of replacement income at a given horizon without investing all assets in retirement bonds. By keeping some of the assets available to invest in equities, they have the potential to reach greater income levels than the minimum, just like portfolio insurance aims to protect a minimum amount of wealth while giving the opportunity to grow beyond.

These strategies are of special interest in goal-based investing because they can be employed to secure *essential goals* while leaving the possibility of reaching *aspirational goals*. As such, their properties are easier to explain to individuals than those of strategies based on the principles of mean-variance portfolio theory. They make use of portfolio insurance methods, with a performance-seeking building block, a goal-hedging portfolio and a dynamic allocation between these two components expressed as a function of a *risk budget*. In the following sections, we explain how to relate the investment rules to the choice of the essential goal. This part of the Element is more technical than the others because portfolio insurance through dynamic strategies requires financial engineering, but the most technical discussions have been relegated to the Appendices.

6.1 The Risk-Return Tradeoff in Goal-Based Investing

6.1.1 Shortcomings of Expected Return and Volatility

Following the work of Markowitz (1952), the standard measure of risk modern portfolio theory is the standard deviation of future returns, and ex ante performance is gauged by the mathematical expectation of these returns. These indicators are mathematically convenient for portfolio optimization, but their relevance in goal-based investing can be questioned. Expected return is often misunderstood by individuals unfamiliar with statistics, precisely because they do not know how to combine it with standard deviation to calculate a confidence interval for future returns. A rule of thumb says that a random variable falls within two standard deviations away from its mean with 95% probability, but it implicitly assumes that the variable in question approximately follows a normal distribution.[43] This assumption is often violated in practice, especially for non-linear payoffs like those encountered in portfolio insurance, and in this

---

[43] A random variable X with mean μ and standard deviation σ has a 95% probability of falling in the range $[\mu - 1.96\sigma, \mu + 1.96\sigma]$. The threshold 2σ is a conservative estimate for the radius of the confidence interval.

case, there is no straightforward translation from the mean and the volatility into a confidence interval.

Standard deviation also has well-known limitations as a measure of risk, if only because it does not make a distinction between upside and downside deviations from the mean. But in common perception, risk is much more identified with *downside risk*, since individuals understand it as the risk of losing money, not as the chance of earning more than expected.

Another limitation of the pair expected return-standard deviation is that it is not immediate to relate to target wealth or consumption levels and to the probabilities of reaching these goals, at least for individuals who are not proficient with financial mathematics and statistical calculus. A typical investor's objective will not be stated as "I would like to earn 7.18% per year on average over the next ten years," but is more likely to be phrased as "I would like to double my wealth within the next ten years." The two phrases are equivalent, since $1.0718^{10} = 2$, but the second one will make more sense to most individuals.

Suppose now that the investor is told by the distributor, "I can offer you a fund with an expected gross return of 2 (equivalently, 7.18% per year) and a standard deviation of 1 at the 10-year horizon, or a fund with an expected return of 1.8 (equivalently, 6.05% per year) and a standard deviation of 0.6." Which one is preferable? Fund #2 has less uncertain outcome than fund #1, but it has also a lower expected return, so no fund dominates the other in the sense of mean-variance portfolio theory. Which one an individual chooses depends on his/her *risk aversion*, a parameter that measures how much expected return an individual is ready to sacrifice to enjoy a reduction in volatility. Problem: risk aversion is not observable and not easily measurable, and psychological tests aiming to discern an individual's attitude toward risk in real life or hypothetical situations do not necessarily give a good picture of his or her willingness to take risks when investing.

A more meaningful metric by which to compare the two funds is their probability to reach the investor's objective, which is to double wealth, or equivalently to earn a 200% gross return. Let R denote the uncertain gross return of the fund. A crude assumption is that R is log-normally distributed with mean μ and variance σ,[44] so that the probability of reaching a target return a is

---

[44] We assume that the logarithm of R, not R itself, has a normal distribution, because $\log R$ can be negative, while R is always positive. Since a normal distribution is unbounded from below, the assumption is less unrealistic for $\log R$ than for R.

$$p = \mathbb{P}(R \geq a)$$
$$= \mathbb{P}(\log R \geq \log a)$$
$$= \mathbb{P}\left(\frac{\log R - \mu}{\sigma} \geq \frac{\log a - \mu}{\sigma}\right)$$
$$= \mathcal{N}\left(\frac{\mu - \log a}{\sigma}\right),$$

where $\mathcal{N}$ denotes the Gaussian cumulative distribution function. Taking $a = 2$, we obtain $p = 90.4\%$ for fund #1 and $p = 96.8\%$ for fund #2. By the success probability criterion, the investor should opt for fund #2.

Although it is too technical to be carried out by individuals who are not proficient with financial mathematics, this analysis is still cursory, because returns are not log-normally distributed, especially when investment products contain explicit or implicit options that bring non-linearities, so that the probability of reaching a goal is not just a function of the mean and the standard deviation of the return distribution. A finer approach to estimating probabilities is to generate many stochastic scenarios for the fund's returns and to calculate the average number of successful scenarios, as in Section 5.5.

6.1.2 Probabilities of Reaching Goals

In goal-based investing, performance is useful to the extent that it helps an individual reach aspirational goals, defined as goals that cannot be secured with current savings. For such goals to be attained, the investment strategy must outperform a benchmark, which is the retirement bond in retirement investing. If the goal was expressed as a target wealth level at the retirement date, the benchmark would be the pure discount bond maturing at retirement. But the expected excess return of the strategy over the benchmark discards too much information on the distribution of relative returns; it is just the mean of this distribution. Probabilities of reaching goals contain more information about the distribution, and they quantify the upside potential of a strategy.

An individual can sort his/her goals in two categories. Aspirational goals cannot be secured, but ideally, they should be reached with the highest probabilities, albeit these probabilities are less than 100%. On the other hand, essential goals are affordable goals that should be secured in all market conditions. So, they should be reached with 100% probability, but this confidence level should be robust to parameter and model assumptions, which can prove wrong ex post. This is a strong requirement, which calls for the use of appropriate risk management techniques as discussed in this section.

6.1.3 The Tradeoff between Protection and Upside Potential

In mean-variance portfolio theory, there is a tradeoff between volatility and expected return. The mean-variance efficient frontier is increasing, meaning that an investor who picks an efficient portfolio has to accept more risk if he/she wishes more expected return. In goal-based investing, risk is the risk of missing essential goals, and success is success in reaching aspirational goals. There is also a tradeoff between the two in the sense that requiring a higher level of protection by raising essential goals dampens the upside potential of the strategy and implies lower chances of reaching aspirational goals.

This tradeoff can be illustrated with simple mathematics, even simpler than those behind mean-variance theory. To see this, consider the buy-and-hold strategy introduced in Section 4.3. At the beginning of accumulation, say date 0, the investor is endowed with an amount of savings equal to W_0, which corresponds to a level of replacement income,

$$ri_0 = \frac{W_0}{\beta_0}.$$

The individual decides that he/she does not want necessarily to secure income cash flows equal to this value in retirement, and that he/she is satisfied by securing only a percentage δ_{ess}, which corresponds to an annual income of

$$ri_{ess} = \delta_{ess} ri_0.$$

Ensuring that savings at retirement will be sufficient to finance this amount of income is an *essential goal* for the investor. To have enough savings to finance more than ri_0 is an *aspirational goal*.

To secure the essential goal, the individual invests $ri_{ess}\beta_0$ in the retirement bond that corresponds to his/her retirement date and the rest in an equity portfolio. Until retirement, which takes place at date T, the portfolio is left buy-and-hold, and no new money is infused into it. Let R_{equ} denote the gross return of equities over the accumulation period. The value of savings at date T is

$$W_T = ri_{ess}\beta_T + [W_0 - ri_{ess}\beta_0] R_{equ},$$

so their purchasing power in terms of replacement income is

$$ri_T = \frac{W_T}{\beta_T}$$
$$= ri_{ess} + \frac{W_0 - ri_{ess}\beta_0}{\beta_T} R_{equ}.$$

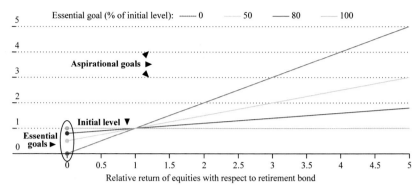

Figure 19 Gross change in the purchasing power of savings in terms of
replacement income during accumulation with a buy-and-hold strategy.
Notes: At the beginning of accumulation, the individual chooses an essential goal,
which is a percentage of the affordable level of income to protect. Savings are invested
in a buy-and-hold portfolio of the retirement bond and equities. Each line represents
the change in the purchasing power in terms of income during accumulation, as a
function of the relative return of equities with respect to the retirement bond.

Letting R_β be the gross return on the retirement bond, we have that the change
with respect to date 0 is

$$\frac{ri_T}{ri_0} = \delta_{ess} + [1 - \delta_{ess}]\frac{R_{equ}}{R_\beta}.$$

Figure 19 depicts the change in the purchasing power in terms of income
as a function of the relative return of equities with respect to the retirement
bond. In all market conditions, the buy-and-hold strategy delivers at least the
minimum amount of income desired by the investor, so it effectively secures the
essential goal. Note that to obtain this result, no assumption is made regarding
the respective expected returns of equities and the retirement bond.

For aspirational goals to be reached, equities have to outperform the retirement bond, and for a given relative return greater than 100%, the level of
income eventually reached is decreasing in the level of the essential goal, summarized in the parameter δ_{ess}. For instance, to multiply purchasing power by
1.5, equities must earn 3.5 times as much as the bond if the essential goal is
set to 80%, but only 2 times as much if the investor is ready to accept a 50%
loss in purchasing power. In the limit case where full protection is required,
savings are entirely invested in the retirement bond, and there is no room for
upside. So, the investor must accept larger losses with respect to his/her current
situation, by setting lower essential goals, to increase the chances of reaching
a given aspirational goal.

6.2 From Optimal to Implementable Strategies

The problem of maximizing the probability of reaching an aspirational goal while securing an essential goal has a straightforward mathematical translation. It can be stated as "maximize the probability of reaching a target wealth level subject to the constraint of respecting a minimum wealth level." In retirement saving, both levels are stochastic because they are proportional to the future retirement bond price. To finance annual income of ri, the individual needs savings of at least $ri\beta_T$. The essential goal is a minimum level ri_{ess}, and the aspirational one is a target ri_{asp}, respectively less than and greater than the currently affordable income level.

6.2.1 Probability-Maximizing Strategy

The probability maximization problem was solved by Browne (1999) and Föllmer and Leukert (1999), and the detailed derivation is presented in Appendix D.1.[45]

To derive the probability-maximizing investment policy, we assume that the market is "dynamically complete," which ensures that any payoff is replicable with a dynamic trading strategy, just like the European call in the Black-Scholes model.[46] In Appendix D.1, we show that under the probability-maximizing strategy, an individual gets the aspirational level of income if, and only if, the *growth-optimal portfolio*, defined as the portfolio that maximizes the expected logarithmic return on savings, outperforms the retirement bond by a threshold h, which can be calculated as a function of the model inputs. When the relative return of the growth-optimal portfolio with respect to the bond is strictly less than h, the individual ends up with insufficient resources to finance the aspirational level of income, but he/she still reaches the essential goal. The growth-optimal portfolio is itself invested in two building blocks, which are the cash account and the maximum Sharpe ratio (MSR) portfolio of all risky assets available.

To find the optimal strategy is equivalent to finding the portfolio strategy that replicates the optimal payoff, like in the option pricing model of Black and Scholes (1973) and Merton (1974). For an analytical expression of the optimal weights to be available, the option price must be known in closed form.

---

[45] The derivation in Appendix D.1 follows the same lines as Föllmer and Leukert (1999) and Browne (1999), but it slightly extends their results by allowing for stochastic minimum and target wealth levels and stochastic investment opportunities, summarized by conditional risk premia, volatilities and correlations.

[46] Technical integrability conditions must be satisfied by the payoff. See Chapter 6 of Duffie (2001a).

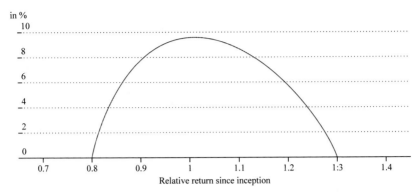

Figure 20 Percentage of wealth allocated to growth-optimal portfolio in probability-maximizing strategy.

Notes: In this figure, the Sharpe ratios of the MSR portfolio and the retirement bond and the volatility of the retirement bond are assumed to be constant. Parameter values are chosen as follows (see Equation (D.11) in Appendix D.1): Sharpe ratio of MSR portfolio $\lambda_{MSR} = 0.6$; Sharpe ratio of retirement bond $\lambda_\beta = 0.3$; annual volatility of retirement bond $\sigma_\beta = 7\%$; time to retirement 10 years; essential level of income $ri_{ess} = 80\%$ of the affordable income level at the beginning of accumulation; aspirational level $ri_{asp} = 130\%$ of the initially affordable income level.

Appendix D.1 explains how to obtain it under the assumption that volatilities, Sharpe ratios and correlations are constant. Remarkably, no assumption on interest rates is needed, and rates can be stochastic. Then, the optimal strategy is to split wealth between the growth-optimal portfolio and the GHP, and the percentage of wealth to be allocated to the former building block is shown to be a function of the distance between current wealth and the minimum amount of wealth to preserve to finance the essential goal. The detailed expression is given in Equation (D.11) of Appendix D.1. Figure 20 shows the optimal fraction of wealth to invest in the growth-optimal portfolio as a function of the relative return of savings with respect to the retirement bond. It is a hump-shaped function of the relative return, which falls to zero at both the essential and the aspirational levels. The property that risk taking vanishes as wealth approaches a floor is standard with portfolio insurance strategies,[47] but the new insight here is that the allocation to the "risky" building block, represented here by the growth-optimal portfolio, also becomes zero when wealth approaches a cap.

While optimal in theory, the probability-maximizing strategy would be hard to implement in practice, due to the discontinuous nature of the payoff, which is

---

[47] See Black and Perold (1992) for constant proportion insurance and Teplá (2001) for option-based insurance.

of the digital type. Moreover, an exact replication strategy is only known under restrictive assumptions ensuring that the option can be priced analytically, and when these conditions are satisfied, the optimal strategy depends on a number of unobservable parameters, including the Sharpe ratios and the volatilities of the risky assets and the retirement bond. More conceptually, the digital payoff may not be appealing to individual investors, who either reach the aspirational goal in full or miss it completely, and switch from success to failure for a small adjustment in terms of the return of the growth-optimal portfolio. Real investors may have more complex preferences than what is implied by the probability maximization criterion, and in cases where they miss the aspirational goal, they are still better off with greater replacement income levels.

These shortcomings motivate the search for simplified versions of the optimal strategy, which would secure a minimum level of income and have growth potential, without using options. This is discussed in more detail in the following section.

6.2.2 Protecting a Minimum Level of Income with Portfolio Insurance

Portfolio insurance is a risk management technique that aims to protect a minimum wealth level while maintaining room for the achievement of higher wealth levels. Indeed, a minimum wealth level at a given horizon can be guaranteed by purchasing a pure discount bond of this specific horizon, but this strategy is pure hedging and it delivers no more than the performance of the pure discount bond, which can be very low if interest rates are low. Instead, portfolio insurance strategies combine a "safe" building block, which is the pure discount bond when the objective is a fixed wealth level, with a performance-seeking one, typically an equity portfolio, so as to reduce the opportunity cost of investing in assets with low expected returns. They can be sorted in two main categories:

- Constant proportion portfolio insurance (CPPI) strategies, in which the dollar allocation to the performance-seeking portfolio (henceforth, PSP) is a multiple of the distance between current wealth and a floor defined as the present value of the minimum wealth level to attain;[48]
- Option-based portfolio insurance (OBPI), which consists of a long position in the PSP and a long position in an "insurance put" written on the PSP. The put insures its owner against the risk of low PSP returns that would compromise the achievement of the essential goal.

---

[48] See Black and Jones (1987) and Black and Perold (1992) for a detailed presentation of these strategies.

Both forms of insurance can be extended to insure a portfolio against the risk of losses relative to a benchmark. In this setting, the objective is to capture some given fraction (80% or 90%) of the performance of a benchmark; rather than attaining a minimum wealth level, the floor is proportional to the value of the benchmark, and the "safe" building block is a benchmark-replicating portfolio. This extension of portfolio insurance is sometimes referred to as "dynamic core-satellite" management:[49] the core is the benchmark-replicating portfolio, and the satellite is the PSP. It can also be used in asset-liability management, when an investor (e.g. a pension fund) wants to respect a minimum funding constraint: the core is the liability-hedging portfolio and the satellite is the PSP. In the extended form of OBPI, the insurance put is replaced with an exchange option between the PSP and the "safe" building block. In both forms of insurance strategies, the pure discount bond is replaced with a *goal-hedging portfolio* (henceforth, GHP) that replicates the present value of the minimum wealth level to attain.

A detailed comparison between the two forms of insurance is beyond the scope of this Element. From a theoretical standpoint, OBPI is optimal for an investor who seeks to maximize expected utility from terminal wealth subject to a minimum wealth constraint, or subject to a minimum funding constraint.[50] For our purposes, it has the inconvenience that it uses exchange options between a PSP and a GHP that would be the retirement bond. These options are not readily available, and their replication raises some of the problems that were already present with the probability-maximizing strategy because unobservable parameters like volatilities are required. For these reasons, we focus on extended forms of CPPI to protect a minimum wealth level.

The building blocks of the strategy are the same as those of modified balanced funds and target date funds (see Section 5.3), namely a PSP and a GHP, intended to replicate the retirement bond. In what follows, we assume that the GHP perfectly replicates the bond. The definition of the floor is determined by the nature of the essential goal. Here, the goal is to reach an essential level of income denoted with ri_{ess}, so the minimum level of wealth to preserve at all times and in all market conditions is the price of the retirement bond that delivers these income cash flows. The dollar allocation to the PSP is taken to be a multiple m of the *risk budget*, defined as the distance between current wealth and the floor. Mathematically, this allocation is given by

$$\theta_t = m[W_t - F_t], \qquad (6.1)$$

[49] See Amenc, Malaise and Martellini (2004) for a description of core-satellite strategies.
[50] See Teplá (2001) and Martellini and Milhau (2012) for proofs of optimality.

where the floor is

$$F_t = ri_{ess}\beta_t.$$

The remainder of the portfolio is invested in the GHP. This strategy has the advantage over the probability-maximizing one that it requires no unobservable volatility or expected return parameter, which should facilitate its implementation.

In the special case where the multiplier is equal to 1, this strategy is buy-and-hold and invests an amount equal to the floor in the retirement bond, and the rest in the PSP. When the multiplier is greater than 1, the strategy involves rebalancing that tends to be procyclical because the percentage allocation to the PSP decreases after the portfolio value has fallen near the floor. It makes intuitive sense that this strategy does secure the essential level of income, because the allocation to the PSP gradually shrinks to zero as portfolio value lands on the floor. Appendix D.2.1 gives a formal proof of this property in the case where the portfolio is *continuously rebalanced* and provides a detailed expression for the level of replacement income attained at the end of accumulation.

6.2.3 Gap Risk and Upside Potential

It is shown in Appendix D.2.1 that the essential goal is secured if the portfolio is continuously rebalanced according to Equation (6.1). In practice, continuous trading is unfeasible, so rebalancing takes place at finite frequencies, typically monthly or quarterly. In this case, the essential goal is only protected if the PSP does not underperform the retirement bond by too large an amount. Indeed, with discrete trading, the readjustment of weights is delayed and can take place after the floor has been breached. Appendix D.2.2 derives a formal result, stating that wealth remains above the floor at all times if, and only if, the gross return on the PSP between two rebalancing dates is at least equal to $1 - 1/m$ times that of the retirement bond. When m equals 1, this condition is always satisfied, and when m grows to infinity, it says that the PSP should always outperform the bond, which is a heavy restriction. For a multiplier of 3, the gross return on the PSP must be at least 66.7% that of the retirement bond.

The advantage of a greater multiplier is that it leads to a larger allocation to the PSP for the same guarantee in terms of minimal income. With the static buy-and-hold approach, the amount of wealth available for investing in the PSP is the excess of wealth over the floor, so it is low if the essential goal is set to a high value and/or the retirement bond is expensive because of low interest rates. The dynamic approach allows the investor to invest less than the present value of the essential goal in the retirement bond, in exchange for a commitment to reduce the exposure to the PSP when wealth approaches the floor.

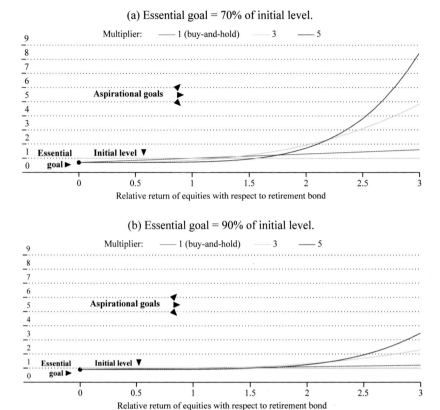

Figure 21 Gross change in the purchasing power of savings in terms of
replacement income during accumulation with a risk-controlled strategy.
Notes: At the beginning of accumulation, the individual chooses an essential goal,
which is a percentage of the affordable level of income to protect. Savings are invested
in a risk-controlled strategy that combines the retirement bond and equities. The dollar
allocation to equities is a multiple of the risk budget, defined as the distance between
current wealth and a floor equal to the price of the retirement bond that delivers the
essential income cash flows. Each line represents the change in the purchasing power
in terms of income during accumulation, as a function of the relative return of equities
with respect to the retirement bond. In this figure, the horizon is set to 10 years and the
tracking error of equities with respect to the retirement bond is assumed to
be 15% per year.

Figure 21 shows the outcome of these risk-controlled strategies, expressed
as the gross change in the purchasing power of savings in terms of replacement
income during the accumulation period. It follows from the calculations in
Appendix D.2.1 that when the portfolio is rebalanced continuously and the
annual tracking error of the PSP with respect to the retirement bond is constant, this change is a function of the relative return of equities with respect
to the bond. The expression is more complicated than for the buy-and-hold

strategy analyzed in Section 6.1 because it is non-linear: indeed, risk-controlled strategies have convex payoffs, which reflect their procyclical nature.

The tension between the objective to cap downside risk and the objective to reach aspirational goals is again apparent. By setting an essential goal to 90% instead of 70% of the initial level of income, one significantly raises the level of outperformance of equities needed to reach ambitious aspirational goals. As a result, the probability of reaching these goals is lower. Interestingly, taking a multiplier greater than 1 does not systematically raise the payoff above the payoff of the buy-and-hold strategy. The threshold is the relative return at which the line corresponding to the greater multiplier crosses the line corresponding to the buy-and-hold strategy, and it can be calculated as shown in Appendix D.2.1. A noteworthy property is that it is independent from the essential goal. With the parameter values assumed in the figure, it is 1.40 for a multiplier of 3, and 1.76 for a multiplier of 5.

Overall, the extended portfolio insurance strategy is an example of a *goal-based investing strategy* because its building blocks and its rebalancing rule are consistent with well-defined goals. It secures an essential goal (up to gap risk), and it has the growth potential needed to reach aspirational goals.

6.2.4 "Monetization" Risk

A corollary of gap risk is the risk of "monetization." In traditional portfolio insurance, monetization occurs when the portfolio becomes fully invested in the risk-free asset, after its value has fallen below the floor. After the risk budget has vanished, the portfolio exactly replicates the performance of the floor, and because it starts from a level less than or equal to the floor, it ends up at the same percentage of the floor value. With continuous rebalancing, this cannot happen, as portfolio value never lands exactly at the floor, and there always remains some risk budget.

In extended portfolio insurance, this risk is still present, but it is the retirement bond that plays the role of the safe asset. If it is observed, at some rebalancing date, that the risk budget is negative, then the allocation to the PSP is automatically set to zero, and the portfolio subsequently replicates the retirement bond. As a result, the probabilities of reaching higher levels of income than at the rebalancing date within the remainder of the accumulation period fall to zero.

In practice, this risk can be mitigated by avoiding violations of the floor in the first place, through a proper choice of the multiplier and the rebalancing frequency. If it materializes anyway, the risk budget can be repleted by resetting the floor to a lower level, so as to recover a non-zero allocation to the PSP and to avoid tracking the returns of the bond. This solution might, however, not be sufficient if the bear market situation persists and the new floor is breached, in which case a new downward reset may be needed. A variant of this approach is to perform resets on a regular basis, as opposed to waiting until the risk budget is exhausted. The strategies introduced in Section 6.3 have such annual floor resets.

6.3 Risk-Controlled Balanced or Target Date Funds

Risk budgeting techniques can be employed to add a risk control layer to standard investment strategies like those of balanced funds and target date funds. This has two advantages. First, the resulting modified strategy can be regarded an evolution of a standard investment policy, rather than as a totally different investment approach like the risk-controlled strategy introduced in Section 6.2. Having balanced funds and target date funds as anchor points should presumably facilitate their adoption by asset managers and distributors. Second, the amendment to the standard investment policy can be done in such a way that the equity allocation of the modified fund matches that of the standard fund on selected dates. This avoids a permanent drift away from the equity allocation chosen as a reference point and ensures that both funds can be compared to each other. In Section 5, we made a minimal change to the design of mutual funds, by changing one building block (the bond index to the retirement bond) and keeping the exact same stock-bond allocation at each point in time. In this section, we move one step further by keeping the same stock-bond allocation at the beginning of every year in accumulation and allowing for deviations from the reference allocation within a year.

6.3.1 Introducing Risk Control in Mutual Funds

As shown in Section 5.5, replacing the standard bond portfolio with the retirement bond of the appropriate maturity in balanced funds and target date funds implies reduced uncertainty over the relative return of the fund with respect to the retirement bond, both in the short run, with lower tracking errors every year, and in the long run, with lower dispersion in relative returns over the entire accumulation period. This means that individuals face less uncertainty over the amount of replacement income that their savings can finance when they retire.

In spite of this improvement, the risk of short-term losses is still present, as illustrated by Figure 22. The year 2008 saw a severe equity bear market, with a loss of 54.7% in the PSP, but sovereign interest rates went down because of flight-to-quality movements during the liquidity crisis, so the retirement bond earned 39.0% in the same year. As a result, equities strongly underperformed the bond, and mutual funds invested in both assets underperformed too, with relative losses of 24.7% and 25.8%, respectively, for the modified balanced

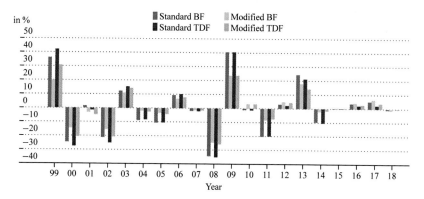

Figure 22 Annual change in the purchasing power of savings in terms of replacement income with mutual funds, from 1999 to 2019.

Notes: The standard funds are invested in an equity index (the S&P 500 index with dividends reinvested) and in a Treasury bond index (the Barclays US Treasury index), and the modified funds are invested in the same equity portfolio and in the retirement bond for an individual who retires in 2019. Balanced funds invest 40% of their assets in equities, and the equity allocation in target date funds decreases from 60% 20 years before retirement to 20% at retirement. Funds are rebalanced every quarter.

fund and the modified target date fund. Comfortingly, losses were larger for the standard funds, and as a general rule, modified funds have less dispersed annual returns, but substantial losses can still occur in the short run.

Reliable protection against the risk of such losses requires a suitable *portfolio insurance* strategy to be set up, similar to the one introduced in Section 6.2. The essential goal to reach here is to cap the annual loss in the purchasing power to a level $1 - \delta$, where δ is a parameter comprised between 0% and 100%. A zero δ means that losses of any arbitrary size are tolerated, while a δ of 100% means that any loss should be avoided. In the former case, the retirement bond is not needed, and in the latter, savings should be fully invested in it. For intermediate values, the portfolio is invested in both assets, according to a risk-controlled investment policy. Because the objective is to keep the purchasing power of savings at the end of the year greater than or equal to δ times its level at the beginning of the year, a floor is formally defined as the price of the retirement bond that pays this amount of replacement income. Mathematically, the floor at date t in year $n + 1$ is

$$F_t = \delta \times \beta_t \times \frac{W_n}{\beta_n},$$

where W denotes the value of savings, β is the bond price, and W_n and β_n denote values at the beginning of year $n + 1$. (W_0 denotes savings at date 0, which is the beginning of year 1, W_1 denotes savings at the beginning of year 2, and so on.) Note that, by definition, the floor equals δ times savings at the beginning of every year.

The dollar allocation to the PSP is taken to be a multiple of the risk budget, defined as the distance between current wealth and a floor. In mathematical notation, it is given by

$$\theta_t = m_n \left[W_t - F_t \right],$$

where m_n is the multiplier for year $n + 1$, fixed at the beginning of the year, which is date n by convention. To make the portfolio comparable to a reference fund, taken to be a standard balanced or target date fund, the multiplier is chosen in such a way that the percentage allocation to the PSP matches the percentage allocation to equities implied by the glidepath. So, we have

$$m_n = \frac{w_{ref,n}}{1 - \delta},$$

where $w_{ref,n}$ is the percentage allocation to equities in the reference fund at the beginning of year $n + 1$. With this specification, the risk-controlled portfolio and the reference fund have the same allocation to equities once a year, and within a year, the equity allocation of the former portfolio is readjusted so as to protect a percentage δ of the purchasing power of savings at the beginning of the year.

This strategy can be regarded as a *risk-controlled* balanced or target date fund, designed to cap annual losses in the purchasing power of savings to a fixed threshold. In the risk-controlled target date fund, it is the multiplier that follows a deterministic glidepath, but the equity allocation varies with the risk budget within a year. An advantage of this approach with respect to the form of risk control introduced in Section 6.2 is that the annual resets avoid the risk of being permanently invested in the retirement bond in case of a violation of the floor within a year. Indeed, the floor is reset back to a percentage of savings at the beginning of every year, so the risk budget on that date is necessarily positive. As a consequence, and even after a breach, the portfolio never remains "monetized" for more than one year.

6.3.2 Historical Backtest

Figure 23 displays the evolution of $100,000 invested in January 1999 in four risk-controlled funds with caps at 20% or 10%. A cap at 20% (resp., 10%) means that the gross return of the strategy over one calendar year, from January to January, should be always 80% (resp., 90%) times that of the retirement bond. In this sample, the retirement bond outperformed equities, with an average annual return of 6.81% versus 5.62% (see Table 3), so the portfolios with higher fractions invested in the bond outperformed the others. Funds with a cap at 90% have a higher floor than those with a cap at 80%, so they tend to have

(a) Value of savings.

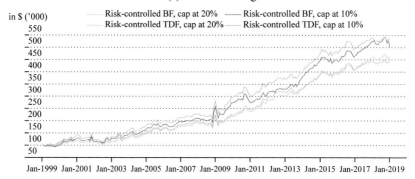

(b) Purchasing power in terms of replacement income.

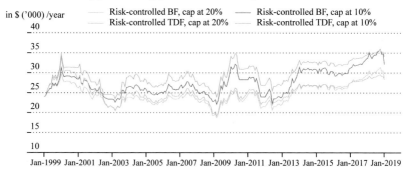

Figure 23 Evolution of $100,000 invested on January 1, 1999 in modified and risk-controlled target date funds, from 1999 to 2019.

Notes: All funds are invested in an equity performance-seeking portfolio, represented by the S&P 500 index, and the retirement bond for an individual who retires in January 2019. They are rebalanced quarterly. They include a risk budgeting mechanism to cap any annual loss in the purchasing power of savings in terms of replacement income. In this figure, some strategies have a cap at 20%, and the others have a cap at 10%. Panel (a) shows the simulated value of $100,000 invested in January 1999, and Panel (b) shows the amount of replacement income that can be financed with savings.

lower risk budgets, and, for a given multiplier, they tend to have lower equity allocations. This explains their outperformance in this particular scenario.

Information on the composition of the funds is provided by Figures 24 and 25. Figure 24 displays the multiplier, which is constant for balanced funds and follows a deterministic glidepath for target date funds. Figure 25 shows the compositions of the two funds with a cap at 20%. By construction, the risk-controlled BF has the same allocation as a standard BF at the beginning of every year, so its composition does not permanently deviate from the 40-60 stock-bond split. Similarly, the equity allocation of the risk-controlled TDF in January always coincides with that of a standard deterministic TDF, so it

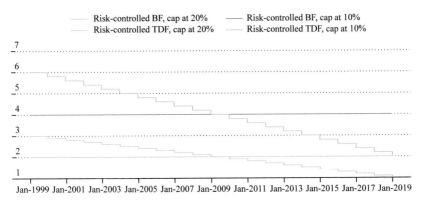

Figure 24 Multipliers of risk-controlled funds, from 1999 to 2019.

Notes: In each risk-controlled fund, the dollar allocation to the equity performance-seeking portfolio is equal to the risk budget, defined as current value minus a floor, times a multiplier. In risk-controlled target date funds, the multiplier is reset every year in January so as to match the percentage allocation to equities of a standard target date fund with a deterministic glidepath (see Figure 15). In risk-controlled balanced funds, the multiplier is constant and set in such a way that the percentage allocation to equities in January of every year is 40%. For both types of funds, the multiplier depends on the maximum relative loss with respect to the retirement bond tolerated. In this figure, the cap is set to 20% or 10%.

decreases from 60% to 20%. But within a year, the equity allocation of every risk-controlled fund moves in response to changes in the portfolio value with respect to the retirement bond. The impacts of the equity bear markets in 2000, 2002, 2008 and 2011 are well visible, with a corresponding reduction in the exposure to equities.

6.3.3 Impact of Rebalancing Frequency on Gap Risk

To check whether the risk control mechanism is effective at capping relative losses with respect to the retirement bond, we plot annual relative returns in Figure 26. With a cap at 20%, no relative return less than -20% is recorded, so the strategy fulfills its duty. With a cap at 10%, the situation is more complicated, since relative returns less than -10% occur in 2001, 2002, 2008 and 2011. In 2002, the BF and the TDF lose respectively 11.39% and 11.42% with respect to the bond, and the worst relative returns are observed in 2011, with -15.27% for the BF and -13.61% for the TDF.

Relative returns less than -10% reveal the existence of gap risk, like for the strategy introduced in Section 6.2. Were portfolios rebalanced continuously, their value would always be above the floor that they are designed to respect, but with discrete rebalancing (here, every quarter), severe underperformance

(a) Balanced fund.

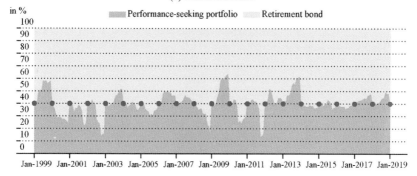

(b) Target date fund.

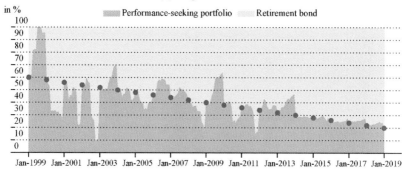

Figure 25 Percentage allocation to building blocks in risk-controlled mutual funds with a cap at 20%, from 1999 to 2019.

Notes: The two funds are invested in an equity performance-seeking portfolio, represented by the S&P 500 index, and the retirement bond for an individual who retires in January 2019. They are rebalanced quarterly. They include a risk budgeting mechanism to cap any annual loss in the purchasing power of savings in terms of replacement income to 20% at the maximum. The figure shows the monthly effective weights, which coincide with post-rebalancing weights in January, April, July and October. Dot markers highlight the January allocation, which, by construction, is always 40% for the risk-controlled balanced fund in Panel (a), and decreases from 60% to 20% for the risk-controlled target date fund in Panel (b).

of equities with respect to the retirement bond can result in violations of this floor. The precise mathematical condition is derived in Appendix D.2.2: for the floor to be respected at all times, the gross return of the PSP within two rebalancing dates must be $[1 - 1/m]$ times that of the retirement bond, where m is the multiplier applied in this period. With a greater multiplier, this threshold is greater, so it is more difficult to attain and gap risk is more likely. This explains why in 2001, only the TDF violates the 10% constraint, with a relative loss of

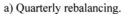

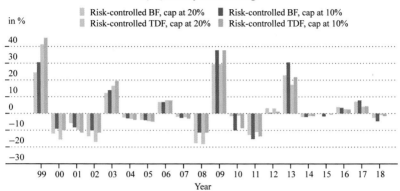

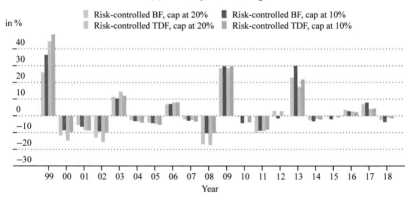

Figure 26 Annual change in the purchasing power of savings in terms of replacement income with a risk control mechanism, from 1999 to 2019.
Notes: All funds are invested in an equity performance-seeking portfolio, represented by the S&P 500 index, and the retirement bond for an individual who retires in January 2019. They follow a risk-controlled strategy designed to cap the annual loss in the purchasing power of savings in terms of replacement income to a predefined threshold, taken to be 20% or 10%. In Panel (a), funds are rebalanced every quarter (in January, April, July and October), and in Panel (b), they are rebalanced every month.

−11.49%, while the BF respects it. Indeed, the TDF has a greater multiplier in early years of accumulation, until 2009 (see Figure 24), so it tends to have a larger equity allocation and is thus more exposed to the risk of a bear market.

The other parameter that impacts the likelihood of gap risk is the rebalancing frequency. With higher frequencies, the returns of the PSP and the retirement bond within one rebalancing period are closer to 1, so the condition of a relative PSP return greater than $[1 - 1/m]$ is easier to satisfy. As a matter of fact, switching from quarterly to monthly rebalancing reduces the magnitude of losses in 2001, 2002, 2008 and 2011. In 2001, 2002 and 2011, both funds with a 10% cap attain their objective, which they missed when they were rebalanced every quarter. A gap is still observed in 2008, with relative returns of −10.34% and −10.36% for the BF and the TDF, but these values are very close to the theoretical threshold of −10%, and they are better than the relative returns of −11.39% and −11.42% that were recorded in the quarterly case.

6.3.4 Stochastic Scenarios

The purpose of the analysis on stochastic scenarios is to study the behavior of the various strategies in many scenarios, to check that they respect the short-term constraints they have been designed to satisfy, and to estimate their respective ex ante probabilities of reaching aspirational goals. This analysis is conducted under the Monte-Carlo simulation model described in Appendix C.1, with interest rate parameters fitted to the US zero-coupon yield curve of January 1, 2019. In other words, the interest rate parameters reflect the conditions of the sovereign fixed-income market at this date.

To gauge the upside potential of each strategy, we construct Figure 27, which shows the level of replacement income attained with 75% probability at each point in the accumulation phase, by investing $100,000 20 years before retirement. We recall that given the possibility of making stop-gain decisions (see Section 5.4), an aspirational goal is said to be reached if there exists at least one date at which savings are in sufficient amount for this goal to be secured: the stop-gain decision is the decision to secure the goal by transferring savings into

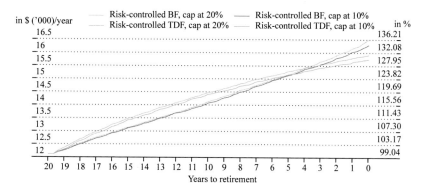

Figure 27 Level of replacement income attained with 75% probability by investing $100,000 20 years before retirement, with January 2019 parameters.
Notes: For each point in the accumulation period and each strategy, the figure displays the level of replacement income attained with 75% probability between the start of accumulation and the point considered. The left axis shows the level of replacement income in $('000) per year, and the right axis expresses this level as a percentage of the initial level.

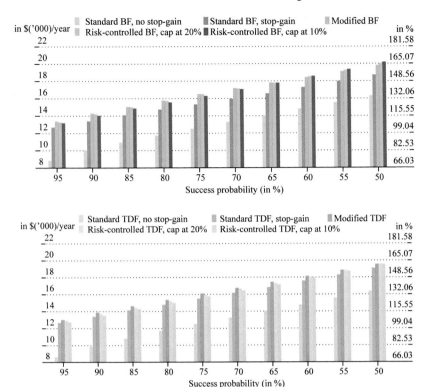

Figure 28 Level of replacement income attained at the end of the accumulation period, by investing $100,000 20 years before retirement. Simulation with January 2019 parameters.

Notes: The left axis shows the replacement income value in $('000) per year, and the right axis expresses these levels as percentages of the initial value, which is $12,116 per year. The standard balanced fund and the standard target date fund are invested in equities and in a bond index, and all other funds are invested in equities and the retirement bond. Modified funds have the same deterministic allocation policy as standard funds, and risk-controlled funds are designed to cap the annual loss relative to the retirement bond to 20% or 10%. Unless otherwise stated, success probabilities are calculated by assuming that the individual can make a stop-gain decision: an income stream can be secured at any point in the accumulation phase by transferring assets into the retirement bond. For standard funds, success probabilities are also reported under the assumption that no stop-gain is possible.

the retirement bond. This figure is visually very close to Figure 18, which shows the same metrics for non-risk-controlled funds. This suggests that the introduction of the risk control does not substantially dampen the upside potential of the strategy.

Figure 28 summarizes the characteristics of the various balanced and target date funds introduced in Sections 5 and 6 in terms of growth potential.

This potential is measured through the income levels reached with probabilities ranging from 50% to 95%. We do not consider goals with lower success probabilities because they are more likely to be missed than to be attained, so that they are not very relevant to investors. At the other end, we refrain from reporting income levels attained in all scenarios, because the phrase "attained with 100% probability" is somewhat misleading: it can be understood as a formal guarantee of success, while the probability is based on a finite set of samples, not on all possible scenarios generated by a model, and, more importantly, it hinges on a model with assumptions and parameter values that can prove wrong ex post.

The first two funds considered are the standard BF, with a 40-60 allocation to equities and a standard bond index, and the standard TDF, which lets the equity allocation decrease from 60% to 20% over the 20-year pre-retirement period. Following the discussion in Section 5.5, we calculate success probabilities for these funds under two alternative assumptions. In the first case, the investor has no access to the retirement bond, so he/she must remain invested in the fund until retirement, even after reaching an income level that looks attractive to him/her. In the second case, he/she can make a stop-gain decision whenever he/she reaches an income level that looks high enough. The former definition is arguably more appropriate for standard funds since they are default investment options in a world where the retirement bond does not exist, but the latter approach allows a fair comparison to be made with the other funds, which include the retirement bond. Modified funds follow the exact same allocation policy as standard funds, but they replace the bond index with the retirement bond. Finally, risk-controlled funds are designed to cap the annual loss relative to the retirement bond to 20% or 10%.

A first observation from Figure 28 is that the three BFs invested in equities and the retirement bond have similar upside potential: for any success probability, the spread between the greatest and the lowest income level is between $42 and $363 per year. For the last three TDFs, the spread ranges from $37 to $386 per year, which is small compared to annual income. Standard funds lag slightly behind in the rather unrealistic situation where stop-gains are possible, and they rank far behind if there are no stop-gains. These observations suggest that matching the equity allocation of risk-controlled funds with that of modified funds once a year through a proper reset of the multiplier helps to ensure that the former funds have comparable abilities to reach aspirational goals.

That risk-controlled funds are close to modified funds, which include no such risk control, may seem surprising because insurance against downside risk should have a cost: these funds should have less upside potential in exchange for avoiding annual losses greater than the prescribed cap. Looking closely at the three BFs using the retirement bond, it appears that is only for the highest success probabilities (70% and above) that this cost is visible, through lower income levels for the risk-controlled funds. At lower confidence levels (65% and below), the opposite holds true, with the latter funds having more growth potential. Among TDFs, the introduction of a risk control has either a slightly negative or a neutral effect on the income level. Overall, insurance against annual losses does have a small negative impact on the chances of reaching "moderately ambitious" aspirational goals, defined as goals reached in 60% or more of scenarios, and a small positive or a neutral impact on the chances of reaching "ambitious" targets, defined as goals reached with probabilities from 50% to about 60%. This can be interpreted by saying that avoiding short-term losses favors the achievement of high goals, or is at least not harmful to it.

6.4 Design Principles of Risk-Controlled Strategies

So far, we have introduced two forms of risk-controlled strategies. Section 6.2 introduces extended portfolio strategies that aim to cap underperformance with respect to the retirement bond to a fixed threshold, and Section 6.3 describes risk-controlled funds, the objective of which is to avoid annual relative returns lower than a threshold. All these strategies belong to a broader class of risk-controlled strategies invested in two building blocks, namely a PSP and the retirement bond, and aiming to avoid exceedingly large losses with respect to the bond. Avoidance of these losses corresponds to an *essential goal* whose achievement is guaranteed by the use of the strategy, up to gap risk. In Section 6.5, we describe several examples of such strategies, which differ in terms of the essential goal.

6.4.1 Mass Customization of Funds

All portfolio strategies that we consider in Section 6.5 are "mass-customized" funds in the sense of Section 5.3. This adjective means that the funds are intended for a large group of people, as opposed to being fully customized. The only customized element is their safe building block, which is the retirement bond. The other building block, the PSP, is the same for all investors.

In addition to their building blocks, all strategies have another common feature, which is the presence of a risk control mechanism whose general purpose is to avoid large downside risk with respect to the retirement bond. This control is achieved by the means of an extended portfolio insurance strategy, with a floor that varies across strategies, depending on how, and over which horizon, relative downside risk is measured. Once a floor has been defined, the risk budget is defined as the current portfolio value minus the floor, and the dollar allocation to the PSP is equal to a multiplier times the risk budget. Mathematically, the percentage weight of the PSP in the portfolio at date t is

$$w_t = m_t \left[1 - \frac{F_t}{X_t} \right], \qquad (6.2)$$

where m_t is the multiplier, F_t is the floor and X_t is the value of one fund's share. This formula can give weights greater than 100%, in case the share's value is much larger than the floor, or negative weights, in the event of a gap, when share's value gets less than the floor. To keep the weight between 0% and 100%, the result of formula (6.2) is floored to 0% and capped to 100%.

Owing to the limited customization constraint, the design of funds cannot involve assumptions on the magnitude of contributions, so the approach is to define strategies regardless of any contribution scheme, and then to check what guarantees they offer to investors. However, to limit the number of funds, strategies that take into account the possibility of periodic contributions within the accumulation period, an assumption can be made on the contribution dates, by postulating that investors bring money at the end or at the beginning of every month or calendar year.

6.4.2 Secured Income Level

It is important for the reporting that comes with goal-based investing strategies to provide investors with a clear view of where they are with respect to their targets. In this regard, it is of particular interest to calculate and report a "secured level" of income, defined as an income value on which the individual can count at retirement, if he/she leaves his/her savings in the same fund and does not make any new contribution. One way to calculate a secured level would be to run a Monte-Carlo simulation of future wealth, by making assumptions on future asset returns and setting future contributions to zero. But, by construction, this value is subject to a number of parametric assumptions, which may be wrong ex post, and it relies on a model for future returns. For these reasons, we reserve such simulations for the estimation of the probabilities of reaching aspirational goals, but we do not use them for the calculation of a secured level.

Formally, a secured level must be a function of quantities known at the reporting date, such as past contributions and past fund's returns, and it should be attained with 100% probability at the end of accumulation if the individual does not contribute after the current date. By absence of arbitrage opportunities, this level is less than or equal to the current affordable income level. Indeed, suppose that at date t, we have calculated a secured level sec_t. So, the income level attained at retirement, at date T, is greater than sec_t with 100% probability. Equivalently, final wealth W_T is greater than $sec_t \beta_T$ with 100% probability, where β_T denotes the bond price just before retirement. By absence of arbitrage opportunities, it follows that the present value of W_T at time t, under the assumption that future contributions are zero, is greater than the current bond price, β_t, multiplied by sec_t. Assuming that the portfolio is self-financed after the current date, the present value of future wealth is current wealth, so W_t is greater than or equal to $sec_t \beta_t$. Equivalently, sec_t is less than or equal to W_t / β_t.

In general, the current income level overstates the secured level because any strategy but the one that is fully invested in the retirement bond has a non-zero probability of underperforming this asset by retirement. But, in general, the risk control implemented in the fund allows one to calculate a lower bound for the relative return of the strategy with respect to the retirement bond. Examples are given in Section 6.5.

6.5 Choose Your Essential Goal

The risk budgeting approach is flexible because it can be adapted to accommodate various forms of performance constraints. In the retirement saving context, it is the performance relative to the retirement bond that is most interesting, because the relative return on a portfolio with respect to this benchmark measures the change in the purchasing power of savings in terms of replacement income. The risk-controlled funds introduced in the previous section essentially focus on short-term relative returns, since their objective is to cap the annual loss relative to the bond to a threshold like 20% or 10%. However, avoiding a "large" downside risk every year does not imply that *long-term* downside risk is controlled. In fact, it is in principle possible – though highly unlikely in practice – to lose 20% with respect to the retirement bond every year, to end up with

$$0.8^{20} = 1.15\%$$

of the initial purchasing power after 20 years. In this extremely unfavorable scenario, the long-term loss is a significant 98.85%.

Of course, a scenario with a 20% relative loss every year for 20 years is an extreme stress test, but this example shows that strategies with different objectives are not substitutes for each other. One that avoids annual relative losses greater than 20% does not avoid 20-year losses greater than this threshold. Conversely, if an investor wants to avoid any long-term loss greater than 20%, he/she does not need to cap annual losses, which would incur unnecessary cost. The purpose of this section is precisely to review various examples of essential goals and to describe risk-controlled strategies that secure these goals.

To make a clear distinction between the values of mass-customized port-folios and the dollar amounts held by investors, we use in what follows the symbol X for the value of one share of a retirement savings fund, and the letter W to denote the accrued savings of an individual. The amount of savings at each point in time depends on the past contributions and the past fund's performance, following the mathematical formulas provided in Appendix B.2.

6.5.1 Essential Goal 1: Secure a Minimum Level of Replacement Income at Terminal Date

Perhaps the simplest floor is the one introduced in Section 6.2: it is defined as the price of the retirement bond that pays some percentage, say 80% or 90%, of the income that is affordable at the beginning of accumulation. Mathematically, if date 0 is the first date of accumulation, β_t is the price at date t of the retirement bond that pays \$1 per year in retirement, δ is the chosen percentage and X_0 denotes the initial share value, the floor at date t is

$$F_t = \delta \times \frac{X_0}{\beta_0} \times \beta_t.$$

The ratio X_0/β_0 represents the income that can be financed at time 0 with one share of the fund.

With this floor, the fund's gross return between date 0 and any date in the accumulation is at least δ times the gross return of the retirement bond. So, savings invested at date 0 benefit from a protection against the risk of a rela-tive loss with respect to the bond: a fraction δ of the purchasing power of these savings is preserved by the retirement date. But contributions made after date 0 do not have the same guarantee because the fund does not take care of rel-ative performance between an intermediate date and the end of accumulation. Appendix D.3 derives an expression for the secured level of income at each point in the accumulation phase, showing that at date t, it is given by

$$sec_t = \delta \frac{R_{X0,t}}{R_{\beta,0,t}} \frac{W_t}{\beta_t}. \tag{6.3}$$

At the retirement date, and in the absence of gap risk, the purchasing power of savings is greater than or equal to the quantity given by Equation (6.3) with 100% probability. The contribution of the money saved at date s to the secured level equals the purchasing power of this money – measured by the ratio e_s/β_s – times δ, times the relative performance of the retirement bond with respect to the fund. As a result, if money is brought after the fund has largely outper-formed the bond, only a small fraction of the purchasing power of this money is preserved.

In this strategy, the multiplier can be taken constant, or it can be adjusted every year so as to match the stock-bond allocation of a balanced or target date fund, as in Section 6.3.

6.5.2 Essential Goal 2: Cap Annual Losses in Purchasing Power

The second class of strategies has a more short-term focus since it aims to avoiding decreases in the purchasing power of savings in terms of replacement income beyond a threshold within a year. The risk-controlled balanced funds and target date funds introduced in Section 6.3 belong to this category.

Assume that cash inflows take place at the beginning of every calendar year, say, on the first day or on the first business day of January. Then, the change in the purchasing power of savings from one contribution date to the next, including the first contribution and excluding the second one, equals the relative return of the fund with respect to the retirement bond between these two dates. So, to avoid any loss in the affordable level of income beyond a cap $1 - \delta$, a necessary and sufficient condition is to ensure that the relative return of the fund within a year is at least δ times that of the bond. For instance, to avoid year-to-year losses greater than 20%, the annual gross return of the fund should be 80% times that of the bond at least, and if the maximum acceptable loss is set to 10%, the minimum relative performance becomes 90%.

To have relative returns greater than δ every year, a risk-controlled strategy with annual floor resets can be employed, as in Section 6.3. At the beginning of every year, the floor is reset back to δ times the current value of one fund's share, and within the year, it replicates the returns of the retirement bond, until the next revision, which takes place at the beginning of the following year. In mathematical notation, the floor at an instant t in year $n + 1$ is given by

$$F_t = \delta \times \frac{X_n}{\beta_n} \times \beta_t,$$

where, by convention, date n denotes the beginning of year $n + 1$, so that date 0 is the beginning of year 1 and so on.

The multiplier can be constant or can be reset every year in order to match the stock-bond allocation of a balanced fund or a target date fund. With the latter option, the strategy becomes one of the risk-controlled balanced funds and target date funds analyzed in Section 6.3.

By focusing on annual changes in the purchasing power of savings, this class of strategies does not allow to calculate immediately a lower bound on the replacement income level attained at the end of accumulation. To estimate a "worst-case" level, one has to consider an extreme situation in which the maximum loss is recorded every year through the accumulation phase. Admittedly, such a chain of bad scenarios is very unlikely under any realistic set of parameter values for asset returns, but it is possible in principle, and to look at this extreme case is the only way to estimate a minimum replacement income without taking a stand on expected returns. The derivation of the secured level is slightly more technical than for the previous strategy, and Appendix D.3 goes through the mathematics. The secured level at date t in accumulation is given by

$$sec_t = \max \left[\sum_{i \leq t} \delta^{T-i} \frac{e_i}{\beta_i}, \max_{i \leq t} \left[\delta^{T-i} \frac{W_i}{\beta_i} \right] \right], \qquad (6.4)$$

where the sum and the maximum are taken over all beginnings of the year preceding date t.

Note that the right-hand side of Equation (6.4) contains quantities of the form δ^{T-i}, where the integer i ranges from 0 to $T-1$. So, the exponent $T-i$ ranges from 1 to T, and for a coefficient δ less than 100%, this quantity rapidly decreases as the number of years grows. For instance, when δ is 80% – meaning that the maximum acceptable annual loss with respect to the retirement bond is 20% – and the contribution takes place 20 years before retirement, the fraction of its purchasing power that is secured with certainty is $0.8^{20} = 1.15\%$. If the contribution takes place one year before retirement, the fraction grows to 80%. In other words, the fraction of the purchasing power of each dollar invested that the investor is certain to recover at retirement strongly depends on the moment the investment is made, and dollars brought many years before retirement have a very small contribution to the secured income level.

6.5.3 Essential Goal 3: Preserve a Fraction of Each Invested Contribution

The third class of strategies aims to address two of the limits of the previous strategies. First, it should secure a fixed fraction of the purchasing power of all contributions, regardless of the time when they are made, while the first form of strategies does not provide a uniform protection: instead, it secures a percentage that depends on the relative return of the fund with respect to the bond between the initial date and the contribution date. The third form of strategies aims to secure a fixed percentage, independent of the moment the contribution is brought.

Second, these strategies have a more long-term objective than those of the second class, which aim to protect some fraction of the purchasing power on an annual basis. Here, the goal is to build up replacement income by adding an increment every time a new dollar is brought into the fund.

Putting the two requirements together, the fund must be such that whenever a dollar is invested, the gross change in the purchasing power of this dollar in terms of replacement income between the investment date and the end of accumulation must be at least equal to a threshold δ. But this change equals the fund's gross return divided by the bond's gross return. So, the fund's gross return between any point of the accumulation phase and the retirement date should be at least δ times that of the bond. Mathematically, if T denotes the retirement date and t is any contribution date, X is the value of one share of the fund and β is the retirement bond price, then it must be the case that

$$\frac{X_T}{X_t} \geq \delta \frac{\beta_T}{\beta_t}.$$

This inequality must hold for *any* contribution date t, so if $\mathcal{A}$ is the set of all possible contribution dates, it is equivalent to have

$$X_T \geq \delta \times \beta_T \times \max_{t \in \mathcal{A}} \frac{X_t}{\beta_t}. \tag{6.5}$$

When new money can be brought at any date, $\mathcal{A}$ is the range of all accumulation dates.

The right-hand side of Equation (6.5) defines a *relative maximum drawdown floor*, which involves the maximum of the fund's relative value during accumulation. More generally, at each point in the accumulation period, the floor is given by

$$F_t = \delta \times \beta_t \times \max_{\substack{s \in \mathcal{A} \\ s \leq t}} \frac{X_s}{\beta_s}.$$

With the allocation rule specified by Equation (6.2) and this definition for the floor, the percentage allocation to the PSP in the fund is at most equal to the current multiplier, m_t, times $1 - \delta$. Thus, if the multiplier is 3 and the maximum relative loss is 20%, then the largest possible PSP allocation is 60%.

Appendix D.3 goes through the calculation of the secured level. At date t in accumulation, the individual knows that, up to gap risk, he/she can count on having the following minimal replacement income at retirement:

$$sec_t = \delta \times \max \left[\sum_{\substack{s \in \mathcal{A} \\ s \leq t}} \frac{e_s}{\beta_s} , \max_{\substack{s \in \mathcal{A} \\ s \leq t}} \frac{W_s}{\beta_s} \right]. \tag{6.6}$$

Recall that W_s denotes the amount of savings at date s. This formula is different from the one in Equation (6.3), which gives the secured level for the first class of strategies, because the investment strategies are different. Thus, different risk-controlled strategies have different implications for individual investors in terms of the secured income levels.

6.5.4 Simulation in Historical Scenario

Figure 29 shows the simulated purchasing power of accrued savings for an individual who would retire on 1 January 2019 and would save $10,000 per year from 1999 to 2018 inclusive. This amounts to a total of 20 contributions

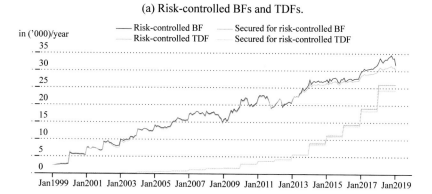

(a) Risk-controlled BFs and TDFs.

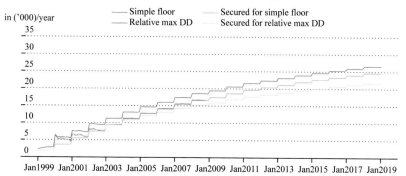

(b) Other risk-controlled strategies.

Figure 29 Purchasing power of savings in terms of replacement income by saving $10,000 every year from January 1999 to January 2019.

Notes: All funds are invested in an equity performance-seeking portfolio and the retirement bond for an investor who retires on January 1, 2019. Risk-controlled balanced funds and target date funds aim to cap the January-to-January loss relative to the retirement bond to 20% at most. Every year, the multiplier of the BF is reset in such a way that the equity allocation is 40%, and the multiplier of the TDF is reset so that the equity allocation matches that of a standard target date fund that starts from 60% in 1999 and ends at 20% in 2019. The "simple floor" strategy aims to capture at least 80% of the performance of the retirement bond over the period from January 1999 to January 2019, and the "relative max DD" one aims to avoid losing more than 20% of the maximum purchasing power measured across past dates. The investor adds $10,000 to his/her savings account at the beginning of every year from 1999 to 2018 inclusive. No contribution takes place in January 2019.

of $10,000 each. Also displayed is the secured level for each strategy, which is by construction less than or equal to the current affordable level as long as the fund does not breach its floor. For each fund, it evolves depending on the realized performance of the fund with respect to the retirement bond and the contributions made. The strategy that secures 80% of the purchasing power of the initial contribution and has no subsequent floor resets is referred to as the "simple floor" strategy. The other three funds involve forms of floor resets.

The $10,000 brought in January 1999 could finance $2,393 per year beginning in 2019. In this sample, it is the two funds with annual floor resets – plotted in Panel (a) – that most efficiently converted regular savings into replacement income, since the BF and the TDF lead respectively to $31,709 and $30,162 per year, versus $24,601 and $26,585 for the strategy with a simple floor and the one with the drawdown constraint. To define a "rate of return" on contributions is not straightforward, given that they are done at different dates, but one can do a back-of-the-envelope calculation by ignoring any discounting effect and by simply comparing the total amount of money brought by the investor, which is $20 \times 10,000 = \$200,000$, and the total amount of money that he/she is entitled to by investing savings in the retirement bond at the start of retirement. Because the accumulation and the decumulation periods happen to be the same duration here, this comparison is equivalent to the comparison between annual savings and the annual replacement income. For each of the four strategies shown here, income is at least 2.46 times as large as savings, so the individual largely benefits from saving money in these funds. In practice, fees will apply and replacement income will be taxed, but a good case can be made that these strategies are an efficient way to convert savings during working years into retirement income.

The last two strategies are penalized by gap risk, which causes them to be completely invested in the retirement bond as of January 2009, as can be seen from Figure 30. This "monetization" occurs after the severe bear market of 2008, in which equities lost 54.7% and the retirement bond earned 39.0% in one year. The strong underperformance of equities within a short time frame caused each strategy to breach its floor, which, according to the rebalancing rule, implies that portfolios become fully invested in the retirement bond. Once equities have been ruled out, the purchasing power of accrued savings only grows by the virtue of fresh money brought by the investor – hence the staircase pattern of the curves in Panel (b). For the strategy with the simple floor, it can be shown that after the monetization date – that is after January 1, 2009 – the ratio of the current affordable income level to the secured level is constant and equal to

$$\frac{1}{0.8} \times \frac{R_{X,\text{Jan-1999,Jan-2009}}}{R_{\beta,\text{Jan-1999,Jan-2009}}}, \qquad (6.7)$$

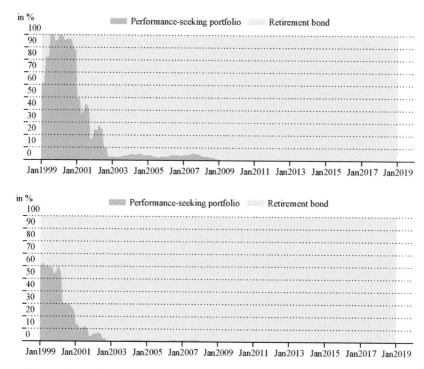

Figure 30 Weights of risk-controlled funds from January 1999 to January 2019, with monetization in January 2009.

where $R_{X,s,t}$ and $R_{\beta,s,t}$ denote respectively the gross return of the fund and the gross return of the retirement bond between dates s and t. Because of the gap in January 2009, the quantity in Equation (6.7) is less than or equal to 1. In this example, it is 0.9992, so the violation of the secured level due to gap risk is limited in size.

The risk-controlled BFs and TDFs are also affected by the bear market, but as can be seen from Figure 26, they keep the relative loss in 2008 under the 20% cap, thanks to a suitable choice of the floor. As a consequence, they are not monetized, as appears from Figure 25. Even if they were monetized within a year after a severe equity bear market, this situation would not be permanent since the equity allocation would be set back to a non-zero value at the start of the next year.

For the strategy with a simple floor, monetization implies that the investor gets no more than the secured level when leaving for retirement. In fact, he/she gets slightly less since the final purchasing power is $24,601 while the secured level is $24,621. The $20 spread illustrates the fact that although the secured level is derived without making assumptions on expected returns and without assuming that any new money will be invested in the future, it is only guaranteed to the extent that the strategy does not violate its floor. Here, a violation occurs in 2008, so the secured level is not attained at the end of accumulation. The lesson from this example is that secured levels should not be presented to investors as formal guarantees and that they should come with disclaimers.

6.5.5 Simulation in Stochastic Scenarios

A Monte-Carlo simulation model allows for a comparison between the expected behaviors of strategies across many scenarios for equity returns and interest rates. In Table 5, we check that each risk-controlled strategy reaches the essential goal that it was designed to reach, up to gap risk. We consider the following three essential goals, henceforth referred to as EG1, EG2 and EG3 in short:

1. The first goal is to keep the final replacement income above the quantity defined by Equation (6.3), calculated with the returns of the fund in which savings are invested. If there were a single inflow of money, at the start of accumulation, this goal would simply be to preserve 80% of the purchasing power of these dollars at the end of accumulation. Our definition of the goal is an extension of this definition, which accounts for the presence of contributions after the initial date. Because the achievement of the goal is checked at the end of accumulation, this goal is said to be "long-term." The next two goals are more short-term in nature.
2. The second goal is to avoid an annual loss in the purchasing power in terms of replacement income greater than 20%. The loss over a given year is measured as the income level at the start of the next year, excluding money brought at this date, divided by the income level at the beginning of the year, minus 1. It is equal to the relative return of the fund with respect to the retirement bond.
3. The third goal is to avoid losing more than 20% of the maximum replacement income across past dates.

By construction, and up to gap risk, EG1 is attained with 100% probability by the strategy with a simple floor, EG2 by the risk-controlled BFs and TDFs, and EG3 by the strategy with a relative maximum drawdown floor. The shortfall probabilities in Table 5 are defined as the probabilities of missing the goals. We also report shortfall indicators to quantify the magnitude of failures caused by gap risk. For EG1, the indicator is calculated by dividing the replacement income level achieved at the retirement date by the quantity in Equation (6.3), also evaluated at the retirement date, and by subtracting the minimum across all

Table 5 Success indicators for essential goals with January 2019 parameters.

	Shortfall probability (%)	Worst shortfall indicator (%)
Essential Goal 1: long-term		
Simple floor	0.02	0.11
Risk-controlled BF	2.54	44.37
Risk-controlled TDF	3.49	50.87
Relative max DD	0.00	0.00
Essential Goal 2: annual loss		
Simple floor	44.34	29.40
Risk-controlled BF	0.00	−3.45
Risk-controlled TDF	0.00	−0.93
Relative max DD	0.00	−0.18
Essential Goal 3: relative drawdown		
Simple floor	61.88	49.02
Risk-controlled BF	1.52	8.11
Risk-controlled TDF	4.59	11.36
Relative max DD	0.00	−0.18

Notes: For EG1, the shortfall probability is the probability for the final income level to be less than the level calculated by Equation (6.3), with a parameter δ equal to 80%. The worst shortfall indicator is 100%, minus the smallest ratio of final income level to the floor given by Equation (6.3). For EG2, the shortfall probability is the probability of experiencing at least one annual loss relative to the retirement bond greater than 20%, and the shortfall indicator is 80% minus the smallest relative annual return across years and scenarios. In the calculation of the annual loss, the contribution made at the beginning of the year is taken into account, but the one made at the start of the next year is not. For EG3, the shortfall probability is the probability of losing more than 20% of the maximum purchasing power attained at previous dates. The shortfall indicator is 80% minus the minimum ratio of the affordable income level to the past maximum. Positive values for shortfall indicators mean that the essential goal is not attained in at least one scenario, so they are associated with positive shortfall probabilities. Zero or negative values mean that the essential goal is attained in all scenarios.

scenarios from 100%. It is 0% if the strategy delivers the income level given by Equation (6.3) in all states of the world. For EG2, the shortfall indicator is 80% minus the worst ratio, across dates and scenarios, of the replacement income level at the beginning of a year, to the level at the start of the previous year. If the annual loss is never greater than 20%, this ratio is nonpositive, and can even be negative if, in all scenarios and all years, the loss is less than 20%. For

EG3, the shortfall indicator has a similar definition, as 80% minus the worst ratio of the income level to the highest income level measured over past dates. If the strategy effectively secures 80% of the maximum income level, this ratio is zero or negative.

The strategy with the simple floor has a 0.02% shortfall probability, which is nonzero because of the quarterly rebalancing frequency. Not only is gap risk small in probability, but it is also small in magnitude, as can be seen from the shortfall indicator, which is 99.89% and is therefore very close to 100%. The risk-controlled BFs and TDFs have small but greater probabilities of missing the long-term goal, but the shortfall indicators are much worse, around 50%. This result means that these strategies cannot be used as reliable proxies for the one with the simple floor. Finally, the relative drawdown fund turns out to achieve EG1 in all scenarios. This may look surprising because this strategy was designed with another essential goal in mind, but this can be explained with Equations (6.3) and (6.6), which give the secured levels for both investment policies. Indeed, it can be shown that the secured income level for the relative drawdown fund, given by Equation (6.6), is greater than the result of Equation (6.3) evaluated with this fund.[51] To the extent that this fund effectively keeps the income level above the minimum written in Equation (6.6), it also reaches EG1.

The next two goals focus on losses with respect to past income levels, either on a year-to-year basis (EG2) or by taking as a reference point the maximum income level attained over past dates (EG3). By construction, the relative drawdown fund should secure both goals, and it does indeed in the simulated scenarios. More surprisingly, the risk-controlled BFs and TDFs have rather low probabilities (less than 5%) of missing EG3, although they are only designed to avoid year-to-year losses greater than 20%.

On the other hand, the strategy with the simple floor has large probabilities of failing to reach EG2 and EG3, at 44.34% and 61.88%, respectively. With this fund, the investor can lose as much as $80 - 29.40 = 50.60\%$ of purchasing power within a year, and $80 - 49.02 = 30.98\%$ of the maximum income level.

From Table 5, it seems that the relative drawdown fund ticks all the boxes, securing the long-term goal and the short-term ones. But it should have in principle less upside potential than the other funds, because its PSP allocation is capped to 60% by construction, while the other funds can allocate up to 100% of their assets to this component. (This 60% is the result of multiplying 3, the

---

[51] To see this, note that the relative drawdown fund satisfies $R_{X,0,s} \geq \delta R_{\beta,0,s}$, so that the quantity defined in Equation (6.3) is less than or equal to $\sum_{s \leq t} e_s / \beta_s$, and is consequently less than the quantity in Equation (6.6).

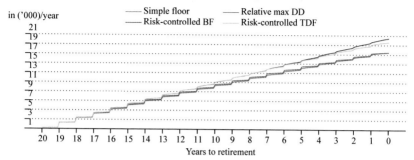

(a) Level attained with 75% probability.

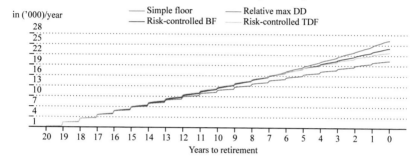

(b) Level attained with 50% probability.

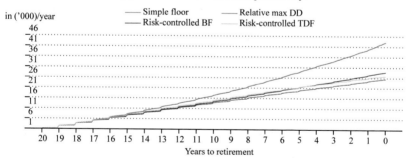

(c) Level attained with 25% probability.

Figure 31 Projection of replacement income level attained by investing saving $10,000 every year for 20 years.

Notes: All funds are invested in an equity performance-seeking portfolio and the retirement bond for an investor who retires at the end of the decumulation period. See the caption of Figure 29 for a description of the strategies and the investor's contribution schedule. The level of replacement income attained with probability x at a date t is the value that the maximum replacement income level between the beginning of accumulation and date t reaches with probability x. In other words, it is the percentile of order $1 - x$ of the distribution of the maximum replacement income between the beginning of accumulation and date t.

multiplier, times the maximum relative drawdown, which is 20%.) To check whether this effect is present in the simulations, Figure 31 displays the quantiles of the maximum replacement income attained within the first 1, 2, . . . , 20 years of accumulation. It turns out that the relative drawdown fund has similar upside potential as the fund with the simple floor for what concerns the level attained with 75% probability: during the 20-year accumulation period, the investor attains respectively $17,452 and $17,487 per year with these two funds.

The advantage of lowering the floor appears when higher target income levels are considered, namely those attained with only 50% or 25% probabilities. With the relative drawdown fund, the individual has 50% chances of being able to finance income of $20,429 per year, but with the simple floor, he/she has the same probability of reaching $26,334 per year. More generally, the ranking of strategies on the "high" projected income levels reflects the intensity of the constraint set on their PSP allocation. The relative drawdown fund is subject to the tightest constraint, since its allocation is capped to 60%, and the risk-controlled BFs and TDFs have a looser constraint, since their allocation is reset once a year to match that of a standard BF or TDF, thereby preventing the possibility of a large PSP allocation for periods exceeding one year. It is in the strategy with the simple floor that the PSP allocation can freely vary up to 100% in scenarios where the fund outperforms the retirement bond, and it is this one that reaches the highest income levels: it offers the possibility of reaching $43,098 per year with 25% probability, but at this confidence level, the other three strategies are under $29,000 per year.

In conclusion, these results provide yet another illustration of the tradeoff between safety and upside potential, as the strategy with the simple floor has the potential to reach ambitious aspirational goals but leaves the possibility of sizable short-term losses, and strategies that avoid losses beyond a certain cap have less chances to result in very high income levels. Comparison between the various forms of risk controls also highlights the flexibility of the risk-budgeting method, which can accommodate different essential goals through a suitable definition of the floor.

7 Conclusion: The Future of Retirement Investing

7.1 Investment Products versus Investment Solutions

Improvement of products has long been a major objective of the investment management industry. Active management has been the dominant paradigm for decades, with the search for alpha in equity funds and the rich-cheap analysis in the fixed-income class. Under this paradigm, to choose a fund means to hunt for the best managers, hoping that their good past track records will persist in the future and that the resulting outperformance will not be eaten by their fees. The situation has been changing since the early 2010s, with the emergence of many new forms of passive products, especially in the equity world, where they are broadly referred to as *smart beta*. Passive investment existed well before, but it was essentially based on the tracking of cap-weighted indices. Drawing on research in portfolio construction and asset pricing conducted since the work of Harry Markowitz in 1952, smart beta aims to provide a better risk-return profile than cap-weighted indices by more efficiently diversifying idiosyncratic risks and by seeking higher exposure to rewarded risk factors. Importantly, these portfolio construction methods rely on systematic security selection and weighting rules, so that they charge much lower fees than traditional active products. In a nutshell, they aim to provide some of the advantages of active funds (i.e. outperform the market) without their shortcomings – their fees and the doubt on performance persistence.

Exchange-traded funds provide investors, including the individual ones, with easy and cheap access to passive strategies, but they do not solve all their problems. After all, a good expected return or Sharpe ratio, a low volatility or a high exposure to a rewarded factor is no guarantee that an investor will have enough money in the future to fund his/her wealth or consumption objectives. Moreover, nothing comes for free, and all these good things come with various sorts of risk: the risk of short-term fluctuations or losses, or uncertainty over the outcome after many years of investing. All these risks can compromise the achievement of essential goals, summarized in minimum wealth or consumption levels to attain, so they should seriously be taken into account. What investors eventually need is *solutions*, which secure their essential goals as reliably as possible and have high probabilities of reaching more ambitious goals, known as aspirational goals.

The design of a genuine investment solution consists in the identification of suitable *building blocks* and an allocation strategy to these blocks. Fund separation theorems from modern portfolio theory suggest that two kinds of blocks at least should be present. A *goal-hedging portfolio* (GHP) tracks the minimum wealth level needed to fund essential goals, a level that varies day to day because of changes in interest rates. The second building block is a *performance-seeking portfolio* (PSP), which is supposed to outperform the GHP in the long run so as to let the investor reach aspirational goals in those scenarios where the expected outperformance materializes. Finally, a well-designed allocation to these blocks ensures that essential goals are secured while maintaining room for outperformance. The last section of this Element demonstrates the flexibility of the concept by showing how differently essential goals can be handled by changing the definition of the floor in a risk-controlled strategy.

A consequence of these guidelines is that investment solutions depend on the nature of the goals. An individual who is in the process of saving for retirement does not have the same goal as another who would like to purchase a property at some given horizon or pay for tuition fees when his/her children begin to attend college. His/her concern is to generate replacement income in retirement, which is different from reaching a fixed amount of wealth and different from tracking property prices or university fees. Moreover, he/she targets income for a specific period beginning at the expected retirement date, so investors with 10 or 20 years to retirement do not have the same needs.

The notion that products should be tailored, to some extent, to an investor's profiles and goals is nothing new. Balanced funds already offer various mixtures of equities and bonds to accommodate different levels of risk aversion, and, closer to the context of retirement, target date funds have a stock-bond allocation that depends on the time to a target date. By taking into account some individualized characteristics, these products represent a first step toward the design of investor-centric solutions, but there are reasons to believe that they still are incomplete, if only because their "safe" building block is a one-size-fits-all bond-cash portfolio that does not guarantee fixed income over the decumulation phase. A key suggestion of this Element is to introduce *retirement bonds*, defined as securities that pay steady income for an individual's expected lifetime beginning at retirement date, and to use them in place of the standard bond portfolio in mutual funds, so as to reduce short-term and long-term uncertainty over the level of replacement income that savings can finance.

Full customization is, of course, impossible for retail clients, who cannot afford mandates. Thus, retirement bonds cannot be offered for each and every possible retirement date, and performance-seeking portfolios cannot be constructed for any underlying investment universe and any diversification method. At the end of the day, building blocks are "mass-customized." Performance portfolios are mutual funds, ideally with low fees, and retirement bonds would be available with a selected number of retirement dates. Individuals would then choose the one with the nearest date to their expected retirement date, as they currently do when they pick a target date fund. Mutual funds that implement a rule-based allocation policy to the building blocks are also necessarily mass-customized, so they should follow strategies that make sense for a broad range of individuals. In the end, the challenge for asset management companies is to provide mass-customized retirement saving solutions with sufficiently low fees to attract savings from many individuals, and to compensate the low income per dollar managed with big volumes.

7.2 The Need for "Goal-Based Reporting" and Better Dialog with Clients

To facilitate the adoption of improved products by their clients, third parties in charge of fund distribution and financial advisors should also adopt a client-centric approach, as opposed to promoting products on the grounds of their alleged qualities, especially on their past returns. As the usual disclaimer goes, past performance is not a reliable predictor of the future, and in any case, past returns do not tell a client whether he/she is far from his/her goals, and similarly, expected returns do not tell how likely he/she is to reach them. In a goal-based perspective, to display the past performance of investment supports over periods of 1, 3 or 5 years is clearly insufficient, even if this basic reporting is completed with risk indicators like volatility and drawdowns. That does not mean that these numbers should be removed from periodic reports and online dashboards, but they should be completed with information on where the client stands with respect to his/her goals.

A first simple metrics to display next to the value of savings is how much replacement income they can finance starting at the client's expected retirement date. This allows the individual to assess his/her current situation with respect to a given target income. The purchasing power of savings in terms of income is obtained as the ratio of savings to the price of a retirement bond that pays $1 every year beginning at the retirement date, and for a period equal to expected lifetime at retirement. Thus, the retirement bond price can be thought of as a price index, similar to the consumer price index but with a focus on the price of replacement income as opposed to the price of goods and services. As such, it should be made publicly and widely available, so that individuals can easily convert the value of their nest egg into a level of income and decide whether or not they need a bigger egg.

The purchasing power of accrued savings tells what goal has been attained to date, but it does not tell how much savings effort and how much performance of the savings account is needed to attain a given target within the remaining accumulation time. It answers the client's question "How far am I from my target?," but the next question is "How do I get there?" A goal-based report could display the probability of reaching the target, subject to assumptions on the future returns on savings, the future interest rates and the future amount of periodic savings. In the absence of a well-specified goal, when the individual simply wants to grow as high as possible, an alternative approach is the one adopted in this Element, which is to calculate the income level that can be reached with 75% probability or any other confidence level.

Digital interfaces can prove extremely useful at this stage, by allowing individuals to simulate the effects of various parameters, including notably those of an increase or a reduction in the future savings effort and those of adopting various investment supports. Information on the probability of reaching a given target should be completed with downside risk indicators, so that individuals realize that strategies with high success probabilities – like investing in stocks – can result in very low replacement income levels in bad scenarios. As a general rule, reporting should give a comprehensive overview of the distribution of outcomes, without hiding the downside, while being concise enough to be understood by non-professional investors. This focused information is crucially needed for individuals to make educated decisions for what regards the various aspects of their retirement preparation.

The next step is to provide investment and savings advice, to guide clients through the forest of investment options and to help them select a good combination of savings amount and investment strategies, which is a more modest and realistic objective than to strike the best mix. This can be done in different ways – for example, by fixing a strategy and by calculating the periodic contribution that allows the target to be reached with a given confidence level (say 75%), or by reasoning with defined contributions and by optimizing over the strategy, or by simultaneously optimizing over both. The theoretical probability-maximizing strategy, which is described in this Element for pedagogic purposes, is not feasible in practice, so search must be performed within a class of strategies. Also, optimization of contributions must be done under the constraint of respecting an individual's savings capacity.

The development of robo-advisors is an opportunity to foster productive dialog with individual clients, by providing interactive dashboards, digital asset allocation tools and automated advice. These platforms can collect information on their clients, including the expected retirement age, the current income and age, and in turn provide customized reporting and advice. In fact, full customization of funds is impossible for retail clients, but in the digital era, customization of reporting based on client's profile is desirable and feasible, since it can be done at minor costs once algorithms and servers are in place.

7.3 Education Challenges

With persisting demographics imbalances, many individuals face the risk of inadequate replacement income, which they need to complete with voluntary savings. It is a task for the asset management industry to improve retirement savings products, and for third parties to move from a product-oriented to a client-oriented approach, but part of the solution to the problem lies in the hands of individuals themselves. It is, after all, their responsibility to decide when to start to save, where to invest, how much to save and how to spend their savings in decumulation.

Economic theory makes a number of prescriptions about how to make welfare-maximizing decisions, but few real-world persons behave like utility maximizers, and solving an intertemporal investment and consumption planning problem remains a difficult task, even for economists. In the absence of scientific guidance, non-professional investors are exposed to a number of pitfalls. The first is the risk of delaying the retirement saving decision and to save too little to favor present consumption. In the investment process, common pitfalls include the blind use of default investment options, the use of heuristics or often-heard rules of thumb, hasty decisions made under emotion and the opposite attitude, namely absence of reaction after a change in the environment. Behavioral finance studies provide a number of examples of these behaviors. Investors tend to stick to default options when they are offered one, such as target date funds in 401(k) plans, and when they are faced with multiple options, they often follow heuristic diversification strategies, dividing wealth equally across a limited number of funds or allocating round numbers (e.g. 50% or 25%) to them.[52] When it comes to decumulation, the "4% spending rule" is still a popular guideline, although it has no rigorous justification as a way to efficiently spend capital without running short of money before the end of decumulation. Behavioral finance has gone a long way toward explaining these behaviors (some of which also affect professional investors) with limited ability to process information, herd instinct and tendency to procrastination, extrapolation and self-confidence.

The goal of financial education is not to teach everyone how to mathematically solve an expected utility maximization problem, but to equip individuals with the tools to understand the implications of their choices. First, people should be aware of the importance of contributing in sufficient amounts and for a sufficiently long time, so as to take the most of interest compounding effects. Second, they should have some minimum knowledge of the properties of financial assets to understand that some are more suited than others for certain purposes. Stocks have historically featured higher long-term returns than bonds, but they have large drawdown risk. Bonds deliver fixed income at least if they are default-free, but not necessarily when this income is needed, and caution should be exercised when considering exotic asset classes owing to

---

[52] See Benartzi and Thaler (2007) for a review of naive diversification strategies typically employed by participants in retirement savings plans.

potentially high fees and lack of hindsight on returns and risk. It is also important to keep in mind the limits of portfolio strategies, in particular for what
concerns their ability to provide replacement income. In this regard, target date
funds are often not understood properly, as appears from a 2012 survey by
Siegel and Gale, in which 30% of respondents say they believe they will get
guaranteed income, while 35% are unsure and the remaining 35% correctly say
that there is, in fact, no guarantee.[53]

A number of initiatives have emerged to raise awareness of these issues and
reduce the undesirable effects of behavioral biases on retirement outcomes.
Thaler and Benartzi (2004) have designed and tested in real companies a "Save
More Tomorrow™" program to commit employees of firms that offer only
defined-contribution plans to increase their retirement saving rates. In 2018,
a French research institute (EDHEC-Risk Institute) and an American university (Princeton) launched a series of "goal-based investing indices," published
on their respective websites, that include the price of retirement bonds, thus
providing a way to calculate the purchasing power of savings in terms of
replacement income. Robo-advisors also have a role to play by making access
to financial information easier and wider. But further initiatives should be taken
to ensure that basic principles for good investment reach the broadest audience,
like recommendations for a healthier condition. To make a comparison, a number of messages have popularized the notion that practicing regular physical
exercise and avoiding tobacco and foods that are exceedingly high in sugar,
fat or salt are key to maintaining good physical condition. To be in good shape
is an asset for a happy retirement, but to have enough resources to sustain an
adequate lifestyle is undoubtedly essential too, so "save regularly and invest
healthily" could be yet another fruitful maxim to follow.

Appendix A to Section 3

A.1 Advantage to Deferring Taxes on Capital Income and Gains

In this appendix, we show that deferring taxes on income and gains from capital
until savings are withdrawn as a lump sum payment leads to greater after-tax
wealth than if taxes are paid periodically.

Consider T periods defined by $T + 1$ dates $0, 1, 2, \ldots, T$, in which the returns
on a financial portfolio are $r_1, r_2, \ldots, r_T$. These returns include any dividends
and coupons, which are assumed to be reinvested in the portfolio, so they are

---

[53] The results of the survey, entitled "Investor Testing of Target Date Retirement Fund (TDF) Com-
prehension and Communications," are available at www.sec.gov/comments/s7-12-10/s71210-
58.pdf.

total returns. They can be positive or negative, but all of them satisfy $r_t > -1$. We want to compare the value of accrued savings at date T in two situations:

- Without a tax deferral: Returns are taxed at rate ρ in every period, where ρ is positive and strictly less than 1.
- With a tax deferral: Returns are not taxed until date T, where they are taxed at rate ρ.

We assume that only positive returns are taxed: a negative return incurs no taxes. Let W_0 be the value of savings at date 0.

Separating out positive and negative returns, the final value of savings without a tax deferral is

$$A = W_0 \left[\prod_{r_t > 0} [1 + r_t[1 - \rho]] \right] \times \prod_{r_t < 0} [1 + r_t].$$

$\prod_{r_t > 0}$, (resp. $\prod_{r_t < 0}$) is a short-hand notation for a product over all periods with a positive (resp. negative) return, with the convention that an empty product equals 1.

If the cumulative before-tax return over the entire period is positive, the after-tax value of savings with a tax deferral is

$$B = W_0[1 - \rho] \prod [1 + r_t] + \rho W_0. \qquad (A.1)$$

If the cumulative return is negative, the after-tax amount of savings becomes

$$B = W_0 \prod [1 + r_t].$$

Of course, B and A are equal whenever ρ is zero or there is a single period.

When the cumulative return is negative, we have

$$B = W_0 \prod_{r_t > 0} [1 + r_t] \times \prod_{r_t < 0} [1 + r_t] \geq W_0 \prod_{r_t > 0} [1 + r_t[1 - \rho]] \times \prod_{r_t < 0} [1 + r_t]$$

$$= A.$$

Consider now the case of a positive cumulative return, so that B is given by (A.1) and there is at least one positive return r_t, and define the function

$$f(x) = \prod_{r_t > 0} [1 + r_t x] \times \prod_{r_t < 0} [1 + r_t],$$

for x in the range $(0, 1)$. The derivative of f is

$$f(x) = \prod_{r_t < 0} [1 + r_t] \times \sum_{r_t > 0} r_t \prod_{\substack{r_s > 0 \\ s \neq t}} [1 + r_s x],$$

which is an increasing function of x. Hence, f is convex, so we have

$$f(\rho \times 0 + [1 - \rho] \times 1) \geq \rho \times f(0) + [1 - \rho] \times f(1).$$

Replacing $f(0)$ and $f(1)$ with their definitions, we obtain

$$\rho \prod_{r_t < 0}[1 + r_t] + [1 - \rho]\prod[1 + r_t] \geq \left[\prod_{r_t > 0}[1 + r_t[1 - \rho]]\right] \times \prod_{r_t < 0}[1 + r_t].$$

The right-hand side is A/W_0. The left-hand side is less than or equal to B/W_0 because

$$\rho \geq \rho \prod_{r_t < 0}[1 + r_t].$$

It follows that

$$\frac{B}{W_0} \geq \frac{A}{W_0}.$$

Hence, B is greater than or equal to A in all cases.

A.2 Spending Rules

In this appendix, we derive the expression for the maximum amount that can be withdrawn every year for τ years from a portfolio whose value at the start of decumulation is W_0. Let c be the annual consumption and W_t be the value of savings before consumption at the end of year t, for $t = 1, \ldots, \tau$.

A.2.1 Constant Rate of Return

We first consider the case where the annual rate of return on savings is a constant r. The budget constraint reads

$$W_{t+1} = [W_t - c][1 + r].$$

It follows that

$$\frac{W_{t+1}}{[1 + r]^{t+1}} - \frac{W_t}{[1 + r]^t} = -\frac{c}{[1 + r]^t}.$$

We obtain, for $r > 0$,

$$\frac{W_t}{[1 + r]^t} = W_0 - c\frac{1 - [1 + r]^{-t}}{1 - [1 + r]^{-1}}. \tag{A.2}$$

The maximum annual withdrawal is such that $W_\tau = 0$, so it is given by

$$c = W_0\frac{1 - [1 + r]^{-1}}{1 - [1 + r]^{-\tau}}.$$

When r shrinks to zero, the numerator is equivalent to r and the denominator to $r\tau$, so c converges to W_0/τ, which is the maximum annual withdrawal when nonconsumed capital produces no interest.

A.2.2 General Case

We now consider the general case, in which the nonconsumed part of savings is invested in a fund whose total return in year t is r_t. Let

$$X_t = \prod_{s=1}^{t}[1 + r_s]$$

be the cumulative return from date 0 to date t, with $X_0 = 1$.

The budget constraint reads

$$W_{t+1} = [W_t - c][1 + r_{t+1}],$$

so

$$\frac{W_{t+1}}{X_{t+1}} = \frac{W_t}{X_t} - \frac{c}{X_t}.$$

Hence,

$$\frac{W_t}{X_t} = W_0 - \sum_{s=0}^{t-1}\frac{c}{X_s}.$$

Wealth at the end of decumulation, W_τ, is nonnegative if, and only if, c is such that

$$\sum_{s=0}^{\tau-1}\frac{c}{X_s} \le W_0,$$

or, equivalently,

$$c \le \frac{W_0}{1 + \sum_{t=1}^{\tau-1}\prod_{s=1}^{t}[1 + r_s]^{-1}}.$$

A.3 Retirement Bonds as the Solution to the Decumulation Problem

Assume that the investor retires at date 0 and plans to withdraw money at dates $1, 2, \ldots, \tau$, with the withdrawal at date t being a fixed multiple of some inflation metrics, y_t. If no cost-of-living adjustment is required, y_t is 1. If a predetermined COLA is applied, y_t grows at a constant rate π, following Equation (4.1), and if the withdrawal is indexed on inflation, y_t is the realized inflation rate between dates 0 and t. We have

$$c_t = ky_t,$$

where k is a constant that must be selected at date 0.

Let M be a pricing kernel for the economy, and denote with $\mathbb{E}_t$ the conditional expectation operator at date t. Savings at the beginning of decumulation are given by

$$
\begin{aligned}
W_0 &= \mathbb{E}_0\left[\sum_{t=1}^{\tau} \frac{M_t}{M_0} c_t\right] + \mathbb{E}_0\left[\frac{M_\tau}{M_0} W_\tau\right] \\
&= k\mathbb{E}_0\left[\sum_{t=1}^{\tau} \frac{M_t}{M_0} y_t\right] + \mathbb{E}_0\left[\frac{M_\tau}{M_0} W_\tau\right] \\
&= k\beta_0 + \mathbb{E}_0\left[\frac{M_\tau}{M_0} W_\tau\right],
\end{aligned}
\tag{A.3}
$$

where β_0 is the retirement bond price at date 0. The highest possible value for k is the one that is compatible with a zero final surplus, so that

$$k = \frac{W_0}{\beta_0}. \tag{A.4}$$

Equation (A.3) also holds just before the first withdrawal:

$$W_{1-} = k\beta_{1-} + \mathbb{E}_1\left[\frac{M_\tau}{M_s} W_\tau\right].$$

Final surplus is always nonnegative, so

$$k\beta_{1-} \le W_{1-},$$

or, equivalently given Equation (A.4),

$$\frac{W_{1-}}{W_0} \ge \frac{\beta_{1-}}{\beta_0}.$$

This equation means that the investor's portfolio must outperform the retirement bond with 100% probability between dates 0 and 1. By absence of arbitrage opportunities, the portfolio must actually have the same return as the bond, so we have, in fact,

$$
\begin{aligned}
W_{1-} &= \frac{\beta_{1-}}{\beta_0} W_0 \\
&= k\beta_{1-}.
\end{aligned}
$$

After date 1 withdrawal, savings become

$$W_1 = W_{1-} - ky_1$$
$$= k\beta_{1-} - ky_1$$
$$= k\beta_1.$$

By induction on the date s, it is shown that for each $s = 0, 1, \ldots, \tau - 1$, the investor's portfolio must be fully invested in the retirement bond over the period from date s to date $s + 1$, and we have

$$W_{s+1} = k\beta_{s+1}.$$

Appendix B to Section 4

B.1 The Nelson-Siegel-Svensson Model

In the Nelson-Siegel model, the zero-coupon curve on a given date is described by the following equation

$$y_{t,h} = \delta_{0,t} + \delta_{1,t} f\left(\frac{h}{m_{1,t}}\right) + \delta_{2,t}\left[f\left(\frac{h}{m_{1,t}}\right) - \exp\left(-\frac{h}{m_{1,t}}\right)\right], \qquad \text{(B.1)}$$

where $\delta_{0,t}, \delta_{1,t}, \delta_{2,t}$ and $m_{1,t}$ are four parameters that depend on time but not on maturity, and the function f is given by

$$f(x) = \frac{1 - \exp(-x)}{x}.$$

The Nelson-Siegel-Svensson extension introduces a fourth term in the right-hand side, equal to

$$\delta_{3,t}\left[f\left(\frac{h}{m_{2,t}}\right) - \exp\left(-\frac{h}{m_{2,t}}\right)\right]. \qquad \text{(B.2)}$$

The coefficients $\delta_{i,t}$ can be interpreted as factor values, as Figure 32 shows. A change in $\delta_{0,t}$ results in a parallel shift of the yield curve since all rates change by the same amount: $\delta_{0,t}$ is a level factor. An increase in $\delta_{1,t}$ results in an increase for all rates, but the change is larger at the short end than at the long end of the curve: the curve flattens, so $\delta_{1,t}$ represents a slope factor. Finally, an increase in $\delta_{2,t}$ leads to a larger increase around average maturities than at the ends of the curve: a convex yield curve (bended downward) gets more convex, and a concave one (bended upward) becomes less concave. This coefficient represents a convexity factor, and the Svensson term (B.2) introduces an additional convexity factor.

To generate a complete term structure by the Nelson-Siegel model, one needs to estimate four parameters – namely the three factor values and the maturity

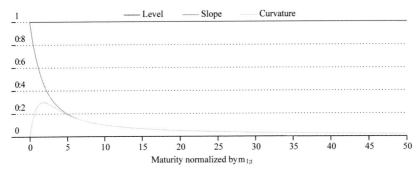

Figure 32 Exposures of zero-coupon rates to changes in factors in the Nelson-Siegel model.

Notes: Factor exposures in the Nelson-Siegel model are measured as the coefficients that multiply the coefficients $\delta_{0,t}$, $\delta_{1,t}$ and $\delta_{2,t}$ in Equation (B.1). The three coefficients are respectively associated with the level, the slope and the curvature factors.

$m_{1,t}$. With the Svensson extension, two additional parameters are needed. For the US, these estimates are available from the Federal Reserve website.

B.2 Investor's Wealth in Accumulation and in Decumulation

This appendix gives mathematical expressions for the amount of savings of an individual in the accumulation and the decumulation phases. The balance of the savings account depends on the investor's decision of how much to save in accumulation and how much to withdraw in decumulation, and also on the returns on the financial portfolio.

Throughout this section, T denotes the retirement date and τ is the length (in years) of the decumulation period. A contribution in accumulation is a cash flow from the outside toward the savings account, while a withdrawal in decumulation is money flowing in the opposite direction. Formally, a contribution can be regarded as a positive cash flow and a withdrawal as a negative cash flow, but for the purpose of clarity, we use the symbol e_t to denote a contribution made at date t, and c_t for a withdrawal, and define both of them to be positive.

W_t is the value of the account at date t, inclusive of the contribution or the withdrawal of this date if money is brought in or withdrawn from the account. The stock of savings just before the cash flow is denoted with W_{t-}, so that we have, if t is a contribution date,

$$W_t = W_{t-} + e_t,$$

and if t is a withdrawal date,

$$W_t = W_{t-} - c_t.$$

B.2.1 General Equations

Wealth in Accumulation Let $\mathcal{A}$ denote the set of contribution dates in accumulation. For each element s of $\mathcal{A}$, the contribution e_s is invested in a fund whose gross return between date s and a subsequent date t is denoted with $R_{s,t}^{(s)}$. The superscript s is introduced for the sake of generality, because contributions of different dates may be invested in different supports. In case the assets the fund is invested in pay coupons or dividends, these are reinvested in the fund, so the gross return must be interpreted as a total return.

Between the date it is brought in and a later date t, a contribution grows from e_s to $e_s R_{s,t}^{(s)}$. Wealth at time t is the sum of the values of past contributions, taking into account the returns on the funds in which they have been invested. So,

$$W_t = \sum_{\substack{s \in \mathcal{A} \\ s \leq t}} e_s R_{s,t}^{(s)}. \tag{B.3}$$

Note the loose inequality in $s \leq t$, which means that the contribution of date t is included. Replacing it with a strict inequality, we obtain the left limit of wealth, which is the value of savings exclusive of the contribution of the current date:

$$W_{t-} = \sum_{\substack{s \in \mathcal{A} \\ s < t}} e_s R_{s,t}^{(s)}.$$

It is assumed that no contribution takes place at the retirement date, so that T does not belong to $\mathcal{A}$.

Wealth in Decumulation At the beginning of decumulation, at date T, the value of savings is W_{T-}. We use the notation W_{T-} instead of W_T because the first withdrawal can take place at date T. The set of all withdrawal dates is denoted with $\mathcal{D}$. Throughout decumulation, savings are invested in a fund whose return between a date s and a later date t is denoted with $R_{s,t}^{(D)}$. Like in accumulation, this return has to be interpreted as a total return, with coupons and dividends reinvested in the fund rather than distributed. This precision is important when the investment support is the retirement bond, because this asset pays coupons.

Wealth at a date t in the decumulation period is given by

$$W_t = W_{T-} R_{T,t}^{(D)} - \sum_{\substack{s \in \mathcal{D} \\ T \leq s \leq t}} c_s R_{s,t}^{(D)}. \tag{B.4}$$

If the first withdrawal occurs at date T, this equation implies that

$$W_T = W_{T-} - c_T,$$

as it should.

A special case of interest is when the annual withdrawal equals the maximum affordable income determined by the value of savings and the retirement bond price at retirement date. At retirement date, and just before the first withdrawal, the purchasing power of savings is, in dollars of date t_0,

$$ri_{T-} = \frac{W_{T-}}{\beta_{T-}}.$$

The withdrawal in year t is

$$c_t = [1 + \pi]^{t-t_0} ri_{T-},$$

so it grows at the annual rate π. If no COLA is applied, withdrawals are constant, but with a positive COLA they grow every year to prevent the purchasing power of spent money in terms of goods and services to be eroded by inflation.

When the investor withdraws the maximum possible amount every year, Equation (B.4) implies

$$W_t = ri_{T-} \left[\beta_{T-} R_{T,t}^{(D)} - \sum_{\substack{s \in D \\ s \leq t}} [1 + \pi]^{s-t_0} R_{s,t}^{(D)} \right]. \tag{B.5}$$

B.2.2 Special Case: 100% in Retirement Bond

Consider the special case in which all savings are invested in the retirement bond. It is the situation considered in the case study of Section 4.4.

Wealth in Accumulation In accumulation, Equation (B.3) gives

$$W_t = \beta_t \sum_{\substack{s \in \mathcal{A} \\ s \leq t}} e_s \frac{1}{\beta_s}.$$

In particular, the maximum affordable goal at time t is given by

$$\frac{W_t}{\beta_t} = \sum_{\substack{s \in \mathcal{A} \\ s \leq t}} \frac{e_s}{\beta_s},$$

which is a piecewise constant function of time: it is constant between two contribution dates.

Total Return on Retirement Bond Care must be taken when applying Equation (B.5) to calculate the value of savings in the decumulation phase, because the retirement bond pays coupons every year. As explained previously, the returns on the investment support that appear in Equation (B.5) are *total* returns, which include reinvestment of coupons. So, we must first calculate the total returns on the retirement bond.

Let $\widetilde{\beta}_t$ denote the total return index at time t. By convention, we take the index value at retirement date to be equal to the bond price just before the first cash flow, β_{T-}, so

$$\widetilde{\beta}_T = \beta_{T-} \tag{B.6}$$
$$= \beta_T + y_T,$$

where y_T is the bond cash flow at date T. A general expression for y_t is given by Equation (4.1), that is

$$y_t = y_{t_0} \times [1 + \pi]^{t - t_0},$$

where t_0 is the reference indexation date and π is the annual COLA. For the retirement bond, we have $y_{t_0} = \$1$.

Consider an integer $k = 0, \ldots, \tau - 1$. For any t in the range $[T+k, T+k+1)$, the total return index is given by

$$\widetilde{\beta}_t = \frac{\widetilde{\beta}_{T+k}}{\beta_{T+k}} \beta_t, \tag{B.7}$$

so that

$$\widetilde{\beta}_{[T+k+1]-} = \frac{\widetilde{\beta}_{T+k}}{\beta_{T+k}} \beta_{[T+k+1]-}$$
$$= \frac{\widetilde{\beta}_{T+k}}{\beta_{T+k}} \left[1 + \frac{y_{T+k+1}}{\beta_{T+k+1}} \right] \beta_{T+k+1}.$$

The total return index is continuous at date $T+k+1$, so $\widetilde{\beta}_{T+k+1} = \widetilde{\beta}_{[T+k+1]-}$, and

$$\frac{\widetilde{\beta}_{T+k+1}}{\beta_{T+k+1}} = \frac{\widetilde{\beta}_{T+k}}{\beta_{T+k}} \left[1 + \frac{y_{T+k+1}}{\beta_{T+k+1}} \right].$$

Hence, we have

$$\frac{\widetilde{\beta}_{T+k}}{\beta_{T+k}} = \prod_{j=0}^{k} \left[1 + \frac{y_{T+j}}{\beta_{T+j}} \right].$$

Substituting back into Equation (B.7), we obtain, for t in $[T+k, T+k+1)$,

$$\widetilde{\beta}_t = \beta_t \prod_{j=0}^{k} \left[1 + \frac{y_{T+j}}{\beta_{T+j}} \right].$$

This equality holds for any $k = 0, \ldots, \tau-1$, so we have, for any t in $[T, T+\tau)$,

$$\widetilde{\beta}_t = \beta_t \prod_{\substack{u \in D \\ T \le u \le t}} \left[1 + \frac{[1 + \pi]^{u-t_0}}{\beta_u} \right]. \tag{B.8}$$

Wealth in Decumulation Equation (B.5) gives the value of savings at date t as

$$W_t = ri_{T-} \left[\beta_{T-} \frac{\widetilde{\beta}_t}{\widetilde{\beta}_T} - \sum_{\substack{s \in D \\ s \le t}} [1 + \pi]^{s-t_0} \frac{\widetilde{\beta}_t}{\widetilde{\beta}_s} \right]. \tag{B.9}$$

With Equations (B.6) and (B.8), it follows that the maximum affordable income at time t, the ratio W_t / β_t, is

$$ri_t = ri_{T-} \left[\prod_{\substack{u \in D \\ T \le u \le t}} \left[1 + \frac{[1 + \pi]^{u-t_0}}{\beta_u} \right] \right.$$

$$\left. - \sum_{\substack{s \in D \\ s \le t}} \frac{[1 + \pi]^{s-t_0}}{\beta_s} \prod_{\substack{u \in D \\ s < u \le t}} \left[1 + \frac{[1 + \pi]^{u-t_0}}{\beta_u} \right] \right]. \tag{B.10}$$

But we have, for any integer n and any real numbers $x_1, \ldots, x_n$,

$$\prod_{i=1}^{n} [1 + x_i] = 1 + \sum_{i=1}^{n} x_i \prod_{j=i+1}^{n} [1 + x_j].$$

Applying this equality with $x_i = [1+\pi]^{u-t_0} / \beta_u$, we ascertain that the bracketed term in the right-hand side of Equation (B.10) is equal to 1. It follows that, for any date t in the decumulation phase, we have

$$ri_t = ri_{T-}.$$

Incidentally, the last equality shows that the expression for wealth in decumulation, Equation (B.9), can be simplified as

$$W_t = ri_{T-} \beta_t.$$

This expression confirms that wealth remains nonnegative throughout decumulation – so that the withdrawal strategy is sustainable – and it is exactly zero after the retirement bond has paid its last cash flow, thus showing that savings are efficiently decumulated since there is no final surplus.

Appendix C to Section 5

C.1 Monte-Carlo Simulation Model

This appendix describes the model used for the generation of multiple stochastic scenarios and the estimation of the probabilities of reaching aspirational goals.

The risk factors involved in the simulation procedure are

- the nominal term structure, which impacts the returns of the goal-hedging portfolio (GHP);
- the value of the stock index used as the performance-seeking portfolio (PSP) in target date funds and risk-controlled goal-based investing strategies; and
- the value of the bond index that serves as a safe building block in standard target date funds.

It is important to note that neither the model nor the associated parameter values are used at any point for the rebalancing of the various strategies or their valuation. They are involved only at the reporting stage, to estimate funding ratio volatilities and the probabilities of reaching various objectives.

C.1.1 Nominal Term Structure

For simplicity, we adopt the one-factor model of the term structure of Vasicek (1977), in which the nominal short-term rate follows a mean-reverting process:

$$\mathrm{d}r_t = a[b - r_t]\,\mathrm{d}t + \sigma_r\,\mathrm{d}z_{rt}.$$

Here, z_r is a standard Brownian motion. In addition to the three parameters in this equation, there are a fourth and a fifth – namely, the price of interest rate risk, λ_r and the initial short-term rate, r_0.

Parameter values are chosen so as to reproduce some of the sample moments of the short-term interest rate and to fit the observed zero-coupon term structure on January 1, 2018. The nominal short-term rate is proxied as the secondary market rate on three-month Treasury bills (www.federalreserve.gov/releases/h15/), and zero-coupon rates of maturities from 1 year to 30 years are downloaded from the Federal Reserve website (www.federalreserve.gov/pubs/feds/2006/200628/200628abs.html).[54] All series are sampled at the daily frequency over the period from January 1998 through January 2018.

---

[54] The zero-coupon rates published on the Fed website are calculated by the method of Gürkaynak, Sack and Wright (2007).

The speed of mean reversion, a, and the short-term volatility, σ_r, are chosen so as to match the historical volatility of daily changes in the short-term rate and the volatility of the short rate level. The sample volatility of daily differences is 77 basis points per year (assuming 260 business days per year), so we take $\sigma_r = 0.77\%$. Rigorously speaking, the model-implied volatility of the change in the state variable over a time step h is

$$\sigma_r \sqrt{\frac{1 - e^{-2ah}}{2a}},$$

but for a very short time step like one day ($h = 1/260$), the correction due to mean reversion is negligible.

The sample volatility of the short rate is 2.00%, and the long-term volatility of the short-term rate in the Vasicek model is $\sigma_r/[\sqrt{2a}]$, so we take $a = 0.0777$. The long-term mean b is taken to be the sample mean of the short rate; hence $b = 0.0176$.

The last two parameters, r_0 and λ_r, are estimated conditionally on the previous ones by minimizing the sum of squared differences between the observed zero-coupon rates and the model-implied rates of maturities 3 months, 1 year and 5, 10, 20 and 30 years on January 1, 2018 (actually, December 29, 2017, which is the latest yield curve available at this date). This implies $r_0 = 0.0239$ and $\lambda_r = -0.005$.

The value of a cash account is simulated as

$$S_{0,t+1} = S_{0,t} \times \exp\left[1 + \frac{r_t}{12}\right],$$

where the time step is one month; hence the factor $1/12$. The initial value is 1, so $S_{0,t}$ is the value of one dollar reinvested every month at the prevailing short-term rate.

C.1.2 *Equity and Bond Indices*

The equity and the bond indices are assumed to have constant volatilities and constant risk premia above the short-term interest rate. Denote their respective values with S and B, so the evolution of S and B is given by the following stochastic differential equations:

$$\frac{dS_t}{S_t} = [r_t + \sigma_S \lambda_S]\, dt + \sigma_S\, dz_{S,t}$$

$$\frac{dB_t}{B_t} = [r_t + \sigma_B \lambda_B]\, dt + \sigma_B\, dz_{B,t}.$$

Here, z_S and z_B are two Brownian motions, correlated with each other and with z_r.

In the Vasicek model, all bond returns are perfectly negatively correlated with the short-term rate, so the correlation between z_r and z_B is taken to be $\rho_{Sr} = -1$. This forces the equality $\rho_{Sr} = -\rho_{SB}$. The correlation between S and B is inferred from Merrill Lynch capital market assumptions (CMAs) for 2017, and is taken to be the average of the correlations between US Large Cap Growth, Large Cap Value, Small Cap Growth and Small Cap Value on the one hand, and Government bonds on the other hand. This implies $\rho_{SB} = -14.75\%$.

The volatility and the expected excess return of the stock index are also borrowed from Merrill Lynch's CMAs, and they are set to 16.2% and 6.40%, respectively. This implies a Sharpe ratio of 0.3951.

For the bond index, the Sharpe ratio is just the negative of the price of interest rate risk, as implied by the Vasicek model; hence $\lambda_B = -0.005$. The volatility is set by assuming that the bond index corresponds to a rollover of bonds with a constant maturity of three years. In the Vasicek model, the volatility of this bond portfolio is

$$\sigma_B = \sigma_r \times \frac{1 - e^{-2a\tau}}{2a},$$

with $\tau = 2$ years. The factor $\left[1 - e^{-2a\tau}\right]/[2a]$ is the negative of the beta of the portfolio with respect to the risk factor – namely the short-term rate. With the above interest rate parameters, we obtain $\sigma_B = 1.38\%$, which implies an expected excess return over the short-term rate of 0.30% per year.

Appendix D to Section 6

D.1 Derivation of Probability-Maximizing Strategy

D.1.1 Derivation of Probability-Maximizing Payoff

Notation Uncertainty is represented by a standard probability space $(\Omega, \mathcal{A}, \mathbb{P})$, where Ω is the set of events, $\mathcal{A}$ is a sigma-algebra and $\mathbb{P}$ is a probability measure that models investor's expectations. The time span is the range $[0, T]$, where 0 is the initial date and T is the investment horizon. The probability space supports a standard vector Brownian motion $(\mathbf{z}_t)_{0 \leq t \leq T}$: the dimension of the vector is the number of independent sources of risk. The probability space is also equipped with the filtration $(\mathcal{F}_t)_{0 \leq t \leq T}$ generated by the Brownian motion. Probabilities and expectations conditional on $\mathcal{F}_t$ are denoted with $\mathbb{P}_t$ and $\mathbb{E}_t$, and the unconditional expectation operator is $\mathbb{E}$.

The investment universe consists of N risky securities with prices $S_1, \ldots, S_N$ and a cash account with value S_0. The annualized rate of return on the cash account over the period from t to $t + dt$ is the nominal short-term interest rate,

r_t. The prices of the risky securities follow diffusion processes:

$$\frac{dS_{it}}{S_{it}} = [r_t + \sigma_{it}\lambda_{it}] \, dt + \sigma_{it}' \, d\mathbf{z}_t.$$

In this equation, the scalar σ_{it} is the asset volatility, the vector $\boldsymbol{\sigma}_{it}$ is the vector of exposures to the independent sources of risk and λ_{it} is the Sharpe ratio. Let $\boldsymbol{\sigma}_t$ be the matrix with columns $\boldsymbol{\sigma}_{1t}, \ldots, \boldsymbol{\sigma}_{Nt}$.

We assume that the market is dynamically complete, that is, any payoff satisfying suitable integrability conditions is replicable.[55] By Theorem 6I in Duffie (2001b), this implies that the dimension of the Brownian motion is exactly N. Then, there exists a unique price of risk vector,

$$\boldsymbol{\lambda}_t = \boldsymbol{\sigma}_t \left[\boldsymbol{\sigma}_t'\boldsymbol{\sigma}_t\right]^{-1} \begin{bmatrix} \sigma_{1t}\lambda_{1t} \\ \vdots \\ \sigma_{Nt}\lambda_{Nt} \end{bmatrix}.$$

The price of risk vector is associated the state-price deflator,

$$M_t = \exp\left[-\int_0^t \left[r_s + \frac{\|\boldsymbol{\lambda}_s\|^2}{2}\right] ds - \int_0^t \boldsymbol{\lambda}_s' \, d\mathbf{z}_s\right]. \tag{D.1}$$

Here, $\|\boldsymbol{\lambda}_s\|$ denotes the Euclidian norm of the vector $\boldsymbol{\lambda}_s$.

Budget Constraint and Objective Investor's portfolio is rebalanced continuously. Let θ_{it} the dollar amount invested in security i at date i, $\boldsymbol{\theta}_t$ be the vector containing $\theta_{1t}, \ldots, \theta_{Nt}$, and W_t be investor's wealth. The intertemporal budget constraint reads

$$dW_t = \left[r_t W_t + \boldsymbol{\theta}_t'\boldsymbol{\sigma}_t'\boldsymbol{\lambda}_t\right] dt + \boldsymbol{\theta}_t'\boldsymbol{\sigma}_t' \, d\mathbf{z}_t. \tag{D.2}$$

Let β_t be the price of the retirement bond corresponding to investor's retirement date and decumulation period. It is assumed to follow a diffusion process, as

$$\frac{d\beta_t}{\beta_t} = \left[r_t + \sigma_{\beta t}\lambda_{\beta t}\right] dt + \sigma_{\beta t}' \, d\mathbf{z}_t. \tag{D.3}$$

The market completeness assumption implies that there exists a perfect goal-hedging portfolio (GHP) for the retirement bond price.

The investor has an aspirational goal and an essential goal, expressed as replacement income levels ri_{asp} and ri_{ess}. His objective is to maximize the probability of reaching the wealth level $ri_{asp}\beta_T$, which will enable him to finance

---

[55] In Chapter 6I of Duffie (2001b), the payoff must be square-integrable with respect to the measure $\mathbb{P}$.

the aspirational level of income, while securing almost surely the wealth level $ri_{ess}\beta_T$. Formally,

$$\max_{\theta} \mathbb{P}\left[W_T \geq ri_{asp}\beta_T\right], \quad \text{subject to } W_T \geq ri_{ess}\beta_T.$$

The essential goal must be affordable, while the aspirational goal is not, so that initial wealth satisfies

$$ri_{ess}\beta_0 \leq W_0 < ri_{asp}\beta_0. \tag{D.4}$$

Optimal Payoff Our derivation of the optimal payoff follows the lines of Föllmer and Leukert (1999). We first define a change of probability measure, from $\mathbb{P}$ to the probability measure $\mathbb{Q}$ defined as

$$\frac{d\mathbb{Q}}{d\mathbb{P}} = \frac{M_T\beta_T}{\beta_0}.$$

Choose the scalar h in such a way that

$$\mathbb{Q}[E_0] = \frac{W_0 - ri_{ess}\beta_0}{\left[ri_{asp} - ri_{ess}\right]\beta_0}. \tag{D.5}$$

(The right-hand side is in the range $[0, 1]$ by Equation (D.4).) Then, define the event $E_0 = \{hM_T\beta_T \leq \beta_0\}$ and the candidate optimal payoff:

$$X^* = ri_{ess}\beta_T + \left[ri_{asp} - ri_{ess}\right]\beta_T 1_{E_0}. \tag{D.6}$$

The indicator function 1_{E_0} is 1 on E_0 and 0 outside.

The present value of X^* is

$$\mathbb{E}\left[M_T X^*\right] = ri_{ess}\beta_0 + \left[ri_{asp} - ri_{ess}\right]\beta_0\mathbb{Q}[E_0]$$
$$= W_0,$$

so, by the market completeness assumption, X^* is an attainable payoff. It clearly respects the floor $ri_{ess}\beta_T$, and its success probability (i.e. the probability of reaching the aspirational goal) is

$$\mathbb{Q}\left[X^* \geq ri_{asp}\beta_T\right] = \mathbb{Q}[E_0].$$

Consider now any strategy with a terminal value W_T satisfying $W_T \geq ri_{ess}\beta_T$ almost surely, and let $E = \{W_T \geq ri_{asp}\beta_T\}$ be its success region. We have

$$\mathbb{Q}[E] = \frac{1}{\beta_0}\mathbb{E}[M_T\beta_T 1_E].$$

But on E, it holds that

$$W_T - ri_{ess}\beta_T \geq \left[ri_{asp} - ri_{ess}\right]\beta_T,$$

so that

$$\mathbb{Q}[E] \leq \frac{1}{\beta_0} \times \frac{1}{ri_{asp} - ri_{ess}} \mathbb{E}\left[M_T\left[W_T - ri_{ess}\beta_T\right] 1_E\right]$$

$$\leq \frac{1}{\left[ri_{asp} - ri_{ess}\right]\beta_0} \mathbb{E}\left[M_T\left[W_T - ri_{ess}\beta_T\right]\right]$$

$$= \frac{W_0 - ri_{ess}\beta_0}{\left[ri_{asp} - ri_{ess}\right]\beta_0} = \mathbb{Q}[E_0].$$

By Neyman-Pearson's lemma, it follows that $\mathbb{P}[E] \leq \mathbb{P}[E_0]$, so X^* is the probability-maximizing payoff.

Growth-Optimal Strategy The growth-optimal strategy maximizes the expected logarithmic return on the portfolio at horizon T. Let $\mathbf{w}_t = \boldsymbol{\theta}_t/W_t$ denote the vector of weights. By integrating Equation (D.2), we have, for any admissible strategy,

$$\ln\frac{W_T}{W_0} = \int_0^T \left[r_t + \mathbf{w}_t'\boldsymbol{\sigma}_t'\boldsymbol{\lambda}_t - \frac{\mathbf{w}_t'\boldsymbol{\sigma}_t'\boldsymbol{\sigma}_t\mathbf{w}_t}{2}\right] dt + \int_0^T \mathbf{w}_t'\boldsymbol{\sigma}_t' \, d\mathbf{z}_t, \qquad \text{(D.7)}$$

so

$$\mathbb{E}\left[\ln\frac{W_T}{W_0}\right] = \mathbb{E}\left[\int_0^T \left[r_t + \mathbf{w}_t'\boldsymbol{\sigma}_t'\boldsymbol{\lambda}_t - \frac{\mathbf{w}_t'\boldsymbol{\sigma}_t'\boldsymbol{\sigma}_t\mathbf{w}_t}{2}\right] dt\right].$$

The quantity

$$\mathbf{w}_t'\boldsymbol{\sigma}_t'\boldsymbol{\lambda}_t - \frac{\mathbf{w}_t'\boldsymbol{\sigma}_t'\boldsymbol{\sigma}_t\mathbf{w}_t}{2}$$

is a quadratic function of weights that is maximized for

$$\mathbf{w}_t = \boldsymbol{\sigma}_t^{-1}\boldsymbol{\lambda}_t.$$

This equation defines the growth-optimal strategy. By Equation (D.7), the gross return R_{gro} satisfies

$$\log R_{gro} = \int_0^T \left[r_t + \frac{\|\boldsymbol{\lambda}_t\|^2}{2}\right] dt + \int_0^T \boldsymbol{\lambda}_t' \, d\mathbf{z}_t.$$

Comparing with Equation (D.1), it follows that

$$R_{gro} = \frac{1}{M_T},$$

so that the success region for the optimal payoff is

$$E_0 = \left\{R_{gro} \geq hR_\beta\right\}.$$

D.1.2 Strategy Replicating the Optimal Payoff

The optimal wealth level at date t is

$$W_t^* = \mathbb{E}_t\left[\frac{M_T}{M_t}X^*\right]$$

$$= ri_{ess}\beta_t + \left[ri_{asp} - ri_{ess}\right]\beta_t\mathbb{Q}_t[E_0] \qquad (D.8)$$

$$= ri_{ess}\beta_t + \left[ri_{asp} - ri_{ess}\right]\beta_t\mathbb{Q}_t\left[\log M_T\beta_T \le \log\frac{\beta_0}{h}\right].$$

By Equations (D.1) and (D.3), and given that $\sigma_{\beta t}\lambda_{\beta t} = \sigma'_{\beta t}\lambda_{\beta t}$, we have

$$\log\frac{M_T\beta_T}{M_t\beta_t} = \int_t^T\left[-\frac{\|\sigma_{\beta s}\|^2}{2} - \frac{\|\lambda_s\|^2}{2} + \sigma'_{\beta s}\lambda_{\beta s}\right]ds + \int_t^T\left[\sigma_{\beta s} - \lambda_s\right]'dz_s.$$
$$(D.9)$$

By Girsanov's theorem, the process $dz_s^{\mathbb{Q}} = dz_s + \left[\lambda_s - \sigma_{\beta s}\right]ds$ is a Brownian motion under $\mathbb{Q}$. We have

$$\log\frac{M_T\beta_T}{M_t\beta_t} = \int_t^T\frac{\|\sigma_{\beta s} - \lambda_s\|^2}{2}ds + \int_t^T\left[\sigma_{\beta s} - \lambda_s\right]'dz_s^{\mathbb{Q}}.$$

Assume that the vectors $\sigma_{\beta s}$ and λ_s are deterministic functions of time and let

$$\eta_{t,T} = \sqrt{\int_t^T\|\sigma_{\beta s} - \lambda_s\|^2\,ds}$$

$$= \sqrt{\int_t^T\left[\lambda_{MSR,s}^2 + \sigma_{\beta s}^2 - 2\lambda_{\beta s}\sigma_{\beta s}\right]ds}$$

be the volatility of $\log M_T\beta_T$ conditional on $\mathcal{F}_t$. Conditionally on $\mathcal{F}_t$, $\log M_T\beta_T$ is normally distributed with mean $m_t = \log M_t\beta_t + \eta_{t,T}^2/2$ and variance $\eta_{t,T}^2$, so that

$$\mathbb{Q}_t\left[\log M_T\beta_T \le \log\frac{\beta_0}{h}\right] = \mathcal{N}\left(\frac{1}{\eta_{t,T}}\left[\log\frac{\beta_0}{h} - m_t\right]\right), \qquad (D.10)$$

where $\mathcal{N}$ is the normal cumulative distribution function. Let q_t denote this probability in what follows.

Apply Ito's lemma to Equation (D.8) to identify diffusion terms (i.e. terms in dz_t):

$$dW_t^* = [\cdots]\,dt + ri_{ess}\beta_t\sigma'_{\beta t}\,dz_t + \left[ri_{asp} - ri_{ess}\right]\beta_t q_t\sigma'_{\beta t}\,dz_t$$
$$+ \left[ri_{asp} - ri_{ess}\right]\beta_t n\left(\mathcal{N}^{-1}(q_t)\right)\left[\lambda_t - \sigma_{\beta t}\right]'\,dz_t.$$

Here, n denotes the normal probability density function, and $\mathcal{N}^{-1}$ is the reciprocal of the normal cumulative distribution function.

Let $\mathbf{w}_{\beta t} = \sigma_t^{-1} \sigma_{\beta t}$. This vector contains the weights in risky assets of the portfolio strategy that perfectly replicates the retirement bond. We obtain

$$\boldsymbol{\theta}_t^* = ri_{ess} \beta_t \mathbf{w}_{\beta t} + \left[ri_{asp} - ri_{ess} \right] \beta_t \left[q_t \mathbf{w}_{\beta t} + \frac{n \left(\mathcal{N}^{-1}(q_t) \right)}{\eta_{t,T}} \left[\mathbf{w}_{go,t} - \mathbf{w}_{\beta t} \right] \right].$$

Re-arranging terms, we obtain

$$\boldsymbol{\theta}_t^* = \varphi_t W_t^* \mathbf{w}_{go,t} + [1 - \varphi_t] W_t^* \mathbf{w}_{\beta t},$$

where the percentage fraction of wealth invested in the growth-optimal portfolio is

$$\varphi_t = \frac{\left[ri_{asp} - ri_{ess} \right] \beta_t \, n \left(\mathcal{N}^{-1}(q_t) \right)}{W_t^*} \, \frac{1}{\eta_{t,T}}.$$

By Equation (D.8), the probability q_t can be rewritten as

$$q_t = \frac{W_t^* - ri_{ess} \beta_t}{\left[ri_{asp} - ri_{ess} \right] \beta_t}$$

$$= \frac{F_t - \delta_{ess}}{\delta_{asp} - \delta_{ess}},$$

where $F_t = R_{W,t}/R_{\beta,t}$ is the relative return of the optimal portfolio with respect to the retirement bond between dates 0 and t.

Eventually, we obtain

$$\varphi_t = \frac{\delta_{asp} - \delta_{ess}}{\eta_{t,T} F_t} \, n \left(\mathcal{N}^{-1} \left(\frac{F_t - \delta_{ess}}{\delta_{asp} - \delta_{ess}} \right) \right). \qquad \text{(D.11)}$$

D.1.3 Optimal Success Probability

The optimal success probability is the probability for the optimal wealth level at retirement to be greater than $ri_{asp} \beta_T$. So, it is given by

$$p_t = \mathbb{P}_t \left[X^* \geq ri_{asp} \beta_T \right]$$

$$= \mathbb{P}_t[E_0]$$

$$= \mathbb{P}_t \left[\log M_T \beta_T \leq \log \frac{\beta_0}{h} \right].$$

By Equation (D.9), the random variable $\log M_T \beta_T$ is normally distributed under $\mathbb{P}$ conditional on $\mathcal{F}_t$, with mean $\log M_t \beta_t - \eta_{t,T}^2/2$ and variance $\eta_{t,T}^2$, so

$$p_t = \mathcal{N} \left(\frac{1}{\eta_{t,T}} \left[\log \frac{\beta_0}{h} - \log M_t \beta_t + \frac{1}{2} \eta_{t,T}^2 \right] \right).$$

Take $t = 0$, so that

$$p_0 = \mathcal{N} \left(\frac{1}{\eta_{0,T}} \left[-\log h + \frac{1}{2} \eta_{0,T}^2 \right] \right). \qquad \text{(D.12)}$$

By Equation (D.10), we have

$$\mathbb{Q}\left[\log M_T \beta_T \le \log \frac{\beta_0}{h}\right] = \mathcal{N}\left(\frac{1}{\eta_{0,T}}\left[-\log h - \frac{1}{2}\eta_{0,T}^2\right]\right),$$

and the left-hand side is by definition equal to the right-hand side of Equation (D.5). Therefore,

$$\frac{1}{\eta_{0,T}}\left[-\log h - \frac{1}{2}\eta_{0,T}^2\right] = \mathcal{N}^{-1}\left(\frac{W_0 - ri_{ess}\beta_0}{[ri_{asp} - ri_{ess}]\beta_0}\right).$$

Substitute back into (D.12) and write the essential and the aspirational levels of income as $ri_{ess} = \delta_{ess} W_0/\beta_0$ and $ri_{asp} = \delta_{asp} W_0/\beta_0$. Then,

$$p_0 = \mathcal{N}\left(\mathcal{N}^{-1}\left(\frac{1 - \delta_{ess}}{\delta_{asp} - \delta_{ess}}\right) + \eta_{0,T}\right).$$

D.2 Extended Constant Proportion Portfolio Insurance

D.2.1 In Continuous Time

Notation The framework is a standard continuous-time model. A probability space $(\Omega, \mathcal{A}, \mathbb{P})$ is given, where Ω is the set of possible outcomes, $\mathcal{A}$ is a sigma-field and $\mathbb{P}$ is a probability measure representing the investor's beliefs about the likelihood of future events. The time span is the continuous range $[0, T]$, where 0 is the initial date and T is the retirement date, and the probability space is equipped with a d-dimensional vector Brownian motion $\mathbf{z}$ representing all relevant sources of uncertainty: this includes uncertainty over security prices, but also uncertainty over interest rates, risk premia, volatilities, correlations and any other parameter of interest. As a result, there may be more sources of uncertainty than traded securities – a situation that characterizes market incompleteness.

The floor is the price of the retirement bond that delivers the essential income cash flows in retirement, so that $F_t = ri_{ess}\beta_t$, where ri_{ess} is the essential annual income amount and β_t is the price of the retirement bond with unit cash flows. The floor at date T is still stochastic because the bond price at the retirement date is uncertain. We assume that the retirement bond follows the diffusion process

$$\frac{d\beta_t}{\beta_t} = \mu_{\beta_t}\,dt + \sigma_{\beta_t}\,dz_{\beta_t}, \tag{D.13}$$

where μ_{β_t} and σ_{β_t} can be stochastic. The returns on the bond are perfectly replicated by a goal-hedging portfolio (GHP).

The second building block of the strategy is a performance-seeking portfolio (PSP), whose value also follows a diffusion process:

$$\frac{\mathrm{d}S_t}{S_t} = \mu_{St}\,\mathrm{d}t + \sigma_{St}\,\mathrm{d}z_{St}. \qquad (D.14)$$

Again, parameters can be stochastic, and even the correlation between the Brownian motions z_F and z_S can be stochastic.

Evolution of Risk Budget The dollar allocation to the PSP at date t is $m[W_t - F_t]$, where m is the constant multiplier and W_t is current wealth. Hence, the intertemporal budget constraint reads

$$\mathrm{d}W_t = m\,[W_t - F_t]\,\frac{\mathrm{d}S_t}{S_t} + [W_t - m\,[W_t - F_t]]\,\frac{\mathrm{d}F_t}{F_t}.$$

Subtracting $\mathrm{d}F_t$ from both sides, and using the fact that F and β are proportional, we obtain the dynamic evolution of the risk budget, $RB = W - F$, as

$$\mathrm{d}RB_t = mRB_t\,\frac{\mathrm{d}S_t}{S_t} + [1 - m]RB_t\,\frac{\mathrm{d}\beta_t}{\beta_t},$$

or, equivalently,

$$\mathrm{d}RB_t = RB_t\left[m\mu_{St} + [1-m]\mu_{\beta t}\right]\mathrm{d}t + RB_t\left[m\sigma_{St}\,\mathrm{d}z_{St} + [1-m]\sigma_{\beta t}\,\mathrm{d}z_{\beta t}\right].$$

Let $\sigma_{S\beta,u}$ be the instantaneous covariance between the PSP returns and the innovations to the retirement bond. By integrating this equation from date 0 to date t, we obtain

$$RB_t = RB_0 \exp\left[\int_0^t \left[m\mu_{Su} + [1-m]\mu_{\beta u}\right]\mathrm{d}u \right.$$
$$\left. -\frac{1}{2}\int_0^t \left[m^2\sigma_{Su}^2 + [1-m]^2\sigma_{\beta u}^2\right]\mathrm{d}u - \int_0^t m[1-m]\sigma_{S\beta,u}\,\mathrm{d}u\right]. \qquad (D.15)$$

Moreover, we have

$$\frac{S_t}{S_0} = \exp\left[\int_0^t \left[\mu_{Su} - \frac{\sigma_{Su}^2}{2}\right]\mathrm{d}u + \int_0^t \sigma_{Su}\,\mathrm{d}z_{Su}\right],$$

and

$$\frac{\beta_t}{\beta_0} = \exp\left[\int_0^t \left[\mu_{\beta u} - \frac{\sigma_{\beta u}^2}{2}\right]\mathrm{d}u + \int_0^t \sigma_{\beta u}\,\mathrm{d}z_{\beta u}\right].$$

Substituting these expressions back into Equation (D.15), we obtain

$$RB_t = RB_0 \left[\frac{S_t}{S_0}\right]^m \left[\frac{\beta_t}{\beta_0}\right]^{1-m} \exp\left[\frac{1}{2}\int_0^t \left[m\sigma_{Su}^2 + [1-m]\sigma_{\beta u}^2\right] du\right.$$
$$\left. -\frac{1}{2}\int_0^t \left[m^2\sigma_{Su}^2 + [1-m]^2\sigma_{\beta u}^2\right] du - \int_0^t m[1-m]\sigma_{S\beta,u} \, du\right];$$

hence

$$RB_t = RB_0 \left[\frac{S_t}{S_0}\right]^m \left[\frac{\beta_t}{\beta_0}\right]^{1-m} \times \exp\left[-\frac{m[m-1]}{2}\int_0^t \sigma_{S/\beta,u}^2 \, du\right], \qquad (D.16)$$

where $\sigma_{S/\beta,u}$ is the instantaneous tracking error of the PSP with respect to the retirement bond, that is,

$$\sigma_{S/\beta,u} = \sqrt{\sigma_{S,u}^2 + \sigma_{\beta,u}^2 - 2\sigma_{S\beta,u}}.$$

Since the risk budget is positive at the initial date, Equation (D.16) shows that it remains positive at all subsequent dates, so that wealth remains strictly above the floor. Hence, the essential goal is reached.

Change in the Purchasing Power of Savings in Terms of Replacement Income In Equation (D.16), the risk budget can be rewritten as

$$RB_t = W_t - F_t$$
$$= ri_t\beta_t - ri_{ess}\beta_t.$$

Let $\delta_{ess} = ri_{ess}/ri_0$ be the essential goal expressed as a fraction of the initial level of income. Then,

$$RB_t = [ri_t - \delta_{ess}ri_0]\,\beta_t.$$

Substituting this expression back into (D.16), we obtain

$$ri_t = \delta_{ess}ri_0 + [1 - \delta_{ess}]ri_0 \left[\frac{S_t}{S_0}\right]^m \left[\frac{\beta_t}{\beta_0}\right]^{-m} \times \exp\left[-\frac{m[m-1]}{2}\int_0^t \sigma_{S/\beta,u}^2 \, du\right],$$

so that the change in the affordable level of income between dates 0 and t is

$$\frac{ri_t}{ri_0} = \delta_{ess} + [1 - \delta_{ess}]\left[\frac{R_{equ,t}}{R_{\beta,t}}\right]^m \times \exp\left[-\frac{m[m-1]}{2}\int_0^t \sigma_{S/\beta,u}^2 \, du\right], \qquad (D.17)$$

where $R_{equ,t}$ and $R_{\beta,t}$ respectively denote the gross return on equities and the gross return on the retirement bond.

For $m = 1$, Equation (D.17) simplifies to

$$\frac{ri_t}{ri_0} = \delta_{ess} + [1 - \delta_{ess}]\frac{R_{equ,t}}{R_{\beta,t}}.$$

Straightforward algebra shows that the income level attained with $m > 1$ is strictly greater than the level attained with $m = 1$ if, and only if, the relative return of equities with respect to the retirement bond satisfies

$$\frac{R_{equ,t}}{R_{\beta,t}} > \exp\left[\frac{m}{2}\int_0^t \sigma_{S/\beta,u}^2\, du\right].$$

Remarkably, the threshold in the right-hand side is independent from the essential goal.

D.2.2 In Discrete Time

Let t and $t + 1$ be two consecutive rebalancing dates. The evolution of wealth over the period from t to $t + 1$ is given by the budget constraint:

$$W_{t+1} = m\,[W_t - F_t]\,\frac{S_{t+1}}{S_t} + [W_t - m\,[W_t - F_t]]\,\frac{F_{t+1}}{F_t}.$$

Rewrite the dollar allocation to the GHP as

$$W_t - m\,[W_t - F_t] = [1 - m]\,[W_t - F_t] + F_t.$$

We obtain

$$W_{t+1} = F_{t+1} + [W_t - F_t] \times \left[m\frac{S_{t+1}}{S_t} + [1 - m]\frac{F_{t+1}}{F_t}\right].$$

Assume that the strategy respects the floor at date t. If $W_t = F_t$, then we have $W_{t+1} = F_{t+1}$, and, by induction on the rebalancing dates, it can be verified that $W_u = F_u$ for all date u in the range $[t, T]$; this means that the portfolio is "sterilized."

Assume now that $W_t > F_t$. Then, wealth is greater than or equal to the floor at date $t + 1$ if, and only if, the returns to the PSP and the GHP satisfy

$$m\frac{S_{t+1}}{S_t} + [1 - m]\frac{F_{t+1}}{F_t} \geq 0,$$

which is equivalent to having

$$\frac{S_{t+1}}{S_t} \geq \left[1 - \frac{1}{m}\right]\frac{F_{t+1}}{F_t}. \tag{D.18}$$

By induction on the rebalancing dates, this discussion shows that if initial wealth is such that $W_0 > F_0$, then Equation (D.18) is a necessary and sufficient condition for the absence of gap risk.

D.3 Secured Income Levels

In this appendix, we derive an expression for the income levels secured by investing in risk-controlled strategies.

For two dates s and t, where $s \leq t$, denote the gross returns of the fund and the retirement bond between these dates with $R_{X,s,t}$ and $R_{\beta,s,t}$. Let $\mathcal{A}$ denote the set of contribution dates in accumulation and e_s be the contribution at date s, for s in $\mathcal{A}$. Then, investor's wealth at time t is given by

$$W_t = \sum_{\substack{s \in \mathcal{A} \\ s \leq t}} e_s R_{X,s,t}, \qquad (D.19)$$

and the affordable level of income is W_t/β_t, which can be rewritten as

$$ri_t = \sum_{\substack{s \in \mathcal{A} \\ s \leq t}} \frac{e_s}{\beta_s} \frac{R_{X,s,t}}{R_{\beta,s,t}}. \qquad (D.20)$$

This equation shows that the annual income that savings of date t can finance is the sum of the annual incomes that past contributions can finance, multiplied by the relative return of the fund with respect to the retirement bond.

D.3.1 Strategy with Simple Floor

This strategy is such that

$$R_{X,0,T} \geq \delta R_{\beta,0,T}. \qquad (D.21)$$

By Equation (D.20), we have

$$ri_T \geq \sum_{\substack{s \in \mathcal{A} \\ s \leq T}} \frac{e_s}{\beta_s} \frac{R_{X,s,T}}{R_{\beta,s,T}}.$$

The right-hand side can be rewritten as

$$\sum_{\substack{s \in \mathcal{A} \\ s \leq T}} \frac{e_s}{\beta_s} \frac{R_{X,s,T}}{R_{\beta,s,T}} = \sum_{\substack{s \in \mathcal{A} \\ s \leq T}} \frac{e_s}{\beta_s} \times \frac{R_{X,0,T}}{R_{X,0,s}} \times \frac{R_{\beta,0,s}}{R_{\beta,0,T}},$$

so, by using Equation (D.21),

$$ri_T \geq \delta \sum_{\substack{s \in \mathcal{A} \\ s \leq T}} \frac{e_s}{\beta_s} \times \frac{R_{\beta,0,s}}{R_{X,0,s}}.$$

Setting contributions after date t equal to zero, we obtain the following expression for the secured income level at date t:

$$sec_t = \delta \sum_{\substack{s \in \mathcal{A} \\ s \leq t}} \frac{e_s}{\beta_s} \times \frac{R_{\beta,0,s}}{R_{X,0,s}}. \qquad (D.22)$$

The affordable income level at date t can be rewritten as

$$ri_t = \sum_{s \le t} \frac{e_s}{\beta_s} \frac{R_{X,s,t}}{R_{\beta,s,t}}$$

$$= \sum_{s \le t} \frac{e_s}{\beta_s} \frac{R_{\beta,0,s}}{R_{X,0,s}} \frac{R_{X,0,t}}{R_{\beta,0,t}}$$

$$= \frac{R_{X,0,t}}{R_{\beta,0,t}} \sum_{s \le t} \frac{e_s}{\beta_s} \frac{R_{\beta,0,s}}{R_{X,0,s}}.$$

By Equation (D.22), it follows that

$$ri_t = \frac{R_{X,0,t}}{R_{\beta,0,t}} \frac{sec_t}{\delta}. \tag{D.23}$$

Suppose that at some rebalancing date u, the fund gets "monetized." This means that, at that date, the fund share's value is less than or equal to the floor, so that

$$R_{X,0,u} \le \delta R_{\beta,0,u}. \tag{D.24}$$

As of date u, the fund is fully invested in the retirement bond, so its gross return between date u and any posterior date is the same as that of the bond. Then, Equation (D.23) implies that, for any date $t \ge u$,

$$ri_t = \frac{R_{X,0,u} R_{X,u,t}}{R_{\beta,0,u} R_{\beta,u,t}} \frac{sec_t}{\delta}$$

$$= \frac{R_{X,0,u}}{R_{\beta,0,u}} \frac{sec_t}{\delta}.$$

So, the ratio ri_t/sec_t is constant beginning at the monetization date, and, by Equation (D.24), we have that

$$ri_t \le sec_t.$$

If this inequality is strict, there is a positive probability for the final replacement income to be less than sec_t, for if ri_T is greater than sec_t with 100% probability, W_T is greater than $sec_t \beta_T$ with 100% probability, so W_t is greater than $sec_t \beta_t$ by the absence of arbitrage opportunities. So, a gap between the fund value and the floor during the accumulation period can result in lower replacement income than the secured level, although this level is supposed to be attained in all scenarios.

D.3.2 Strategies with Floor Resets

Consider now a strategy with floor resets at dates $0, 1, \ldots, T-1$, and assume that contributions take place on these dates. For any integer $n \le T-2$, we have

$$R_{X,n,n+1} \ge \delta R_{\beta,n,n+1}, \tag{D.25}$$

so that, for any integer $n \leq T - 1$,

$$R_{X,n,T} \geq \delta^{T-n} R_{\beta,n,T}.$$

By Equation (D.20), it follows that

$$ri_T \geq \sum_{i=0}^{T-1} \delta^{T-i} \frac{e_i}{\beta_i}.$$

Contributions are nonnegative, so we have, for any date $t \leq T$,

$$ri_T \geq \sum_{\substack{s \in A \\ s \leq t}} \delta^{T-i} \frac{e_i}{\beta_i}. \tag{D.26}$$

Moreover, the return on savings between two contribution dates, excluding the second contribution, equals the return on the fund. Mathematically,

$$\frac{W_{[n+1]-}}{W_n} = R_{X,n,n+1},$$

so that Equation (D.25) implies that

$$\frac{W_{[n+1]-}}{W_n} \geq \delta R_{\beta,n,n+1}.$$

The return on savings including the second contribution is even greater, since

$$\frac{W_{n+1}}{W_n} = \frac{W_{[n+1]-} + e_n}{W_n}$$

$$\geq \frac{W_{[n+1]-}}{W_n}.$$

So, we have

$$\frac{W_{n+1}}{\beta_{n+1}} \geq \frac{W_{[n+1]-}}{\beta_{n+1}} \geq \delta \frac{W_n}{\beta_n}.$$

It follows that, for any integer $n \leq T - 1$,

$$\frac{W_T}{\beta_T} \geq \delta^{T-n} \frac{W_n}{\beta_n}.$$

As a result, for any integer $n \leq T - 1$ and any date t in the range $(n, n + 1)$, we have

$$ri_T \geq \max_{i \leq t} \left[\delta^{T-i} \frac{W_i}{\beta_i} \right], \tag{D.27}$$

where the maximum is taken over all integers i less than or equal to t (i.e. all integers from 0 to n, inclusive).

Putting Equations (D.26) and (D.27) together, we obtain that

$$ri_T \geq \max\left[\sum_{\substack{s \in \mathcal{A} \\ s \leq t}} \delta^{T-i}\frac{e_i}{\beta_i}, \ \max_{i \leq t}\left[\delta^{T-i}\frac{W_i}{\beta_i}\right]\right].$$

The right-hand side of this inequality is known at date t, so it provides a measure at this date of the secured income level.

D.3.3 Strategy with Relative Maximum Drawdown Floor

Consider now a strategy that respects a constraint on the relative maximum drawdown. By definition, we have, for any two dates s and t such that $s \in \mathcal{A}$ and $s \leq t$,

$$R_{X,s,t} \geq \delta R_{\beta,s,t}. \tag{D.28}$$

Take two dates $s \leq t$ with $s \in \mathcal{A}$. By Equation (D.20), we have

$$\frac{W_s}{\beta_s} = \sum_{\substack{u \in \mathcal{A} \\ u \leq s}} \frac{e_u}{\beta_u}\frac{R_{X,u,s}}{R_{\beta,u,s}}$$

$$= \sum_{\substack{u \in \mathcal{A} \\ u \leq s}} \frac{e_u}{\beta_u} \times \frac{R_{X,u,t}}{R_{X,s,t}} \times \frac{R_{\beta,s,t}}{R_{\beta,u,t}},$$

so, by Equation (D.28),

$$\frac{W_s}{\beta_s} \leq \frac{1}{\delta} \sum_{\substack{u \in \mathcal{A} \\ u \leq s}} \frac{e_u}{\beta_u}\frac{R_{X,u,t}}{R_{\beta,u,t}}.$$

Contributions are nonnegative, and $s \leq t$, so we have

$$\frac{W_s}{\beta_s} \leq \frac{1}{\delta} \sum_{\substack{u \in \mathcal{A} \\ u \leq t}} \frac{e_u}{\beta_u}\frac{R_{X,u,t}}{R_{\beta,u,t}}.$$

Applying Equation (D.19), we obtain that the right-hand side is equal to $W_t/[\delta\beta_t]$, so we have

$$\delta\frac{W_s}{\beta_s} \leq \frac{W_t}{\beta_t}.$$

This holds for any $s \in \mathcal{A}$ such that $s \leq t$, so we eventually obtain that, for all t,

$$\frac{W_t}{\beta_t} \geq \delta \max_{\substack{s \in \mathcal{A} \\ s \leq t}} \frac{W_s}{\beta_s}. \tag{D.29}$$

This inequality shows that the property of being above the relative maximum drawdown floor, which holds for the fund by construction, is also verified by an investor's wealth.

Another lower bound for the replacement income level can be derived by substituting Equation (D.28) into Equation (D.19). This substitution implies that

$$\frac{W_t}{\beta_t} \geq \delta \sum_{\substack{s \in \mathcal{A} \\ s \leq t}} \frac{e_s}{\beta_s}. \tag{D.30}$$

The right-hand sides of Equations (D.29) and (D.30) are increasing functions of time, so the replacement income level attained at retirement satisfies, for any date t,

$$\frac{W_T}{\beta_T} \geq \delta \times \max \left[\sum_{\substack{s \in \mathcal{A} \\ s \leq t}} \frac{e_s}{\beta_s}, \ \max_{\substack{s \in \mathcal{A} \\ s \leq t}} \frac{W_s}{\beta_s} \right].$$

The right-hand side is the secured level at time t.

References

Amenc, N., R. Deguest, F. Goltz, A. Lodh and E. Shirbini. 2014a. *Risk Allocation, Factor Investing and Smart Beta: Reconciling Innovations in Equity Portfolio Construction*. EDHEC-Risk Institute.

Amenc, N., F. Goltz and A. Grigoriu. 2010. Risk Control through Dynamic Core-Satellite Portfolios of ETFs: Applications to Absolute Return Funds and Tactical Asset Allocation. *Journal of Alternative Investments* 13(2): 47.

Amenc, N., F. Goltz, V. Le Sourd and A. Lodh. 2015. *Alternative Equity Beta Investing: A Survey*. EDHEC-Risk Institute.

Amenc, N., F. Goltz, A. Lodh and L. Martellini. 2014b. Towards Smart Equity Factor Indices: Harvesting Risk Premia without Taking Unrewarded Risks. *Journal of Portfolio Management* 40(4): 106–122.

Amenc, N., F. Goltz, L. Martellini and V. Milhau. 2010. *New Frontiers in Benchmarking and Liability-Driven Investing*. EDHEC-Risk Institute.

Amenc, N., P. Malaise and L. Martellini. 2004. Revisiting Core-Satellite Investing – A Dynamic Model of Relative Risk Management. *Journal of Portfolio Management* 31(1): 64–75.

Anderson, N. and J. Sleath. 2001. *New Estimates of the UK Real and Nominal Yield Curves*. Bank of England.

Benartzi, S. and R. Thaler. 2007. Heuristics and Biases in Retirement Savings Behavior. *Journal of Economic Perspectives* 21(3): 81–104.

Bengen, W. P. 1994. Determining Withdrawal Rates Using Historical Data. *Journal of Financial Planning* 7(4): 171–180.

Benzoni, L., P. Collin-Dufresne and R. Goldstein. 2007. Portfolio Choice over the Life-Cycle When the Stock and Labor Markets Are Cointegrated. *Journal of Finance* 62(5): 2123–2167.

Black, F. and R. Jones. 1987. Simplifying Portfolio Insurance. *Journal of Portfolio Management* 14(1): 48–51.

Black, F. and A. Perold. 1992. Theory of Constant Proportion Portfolio Insurance. *Journal of Economic Dynamics and Control* 16(3): 403–426.

Black, F. and M. Scholes. 1973. The Pricing of Options and Corporate Liabilities. *Journal of Political Economy* 81(3): 637–654.

Blanchet-Scalliet, C., N. El Karoui, M. Jeanblanc and L. Martellini. 2008. Optimal Investment Decisions When Time-Horizon Is Uncertain. *Journal of Mathematical Economics* 44(11): 1100–1113.

Brennan, M. and Y. Xia. 2002. Dynamic Asset Allocation Under Inflation. *Journal of Finance* 57(3): 1201–1238.

Browne, S. 1999. Reaching Goals by a Deadline: Digital Options and Continuous-Time Active Portfolio Management. *Advances in Applied Probability* 31(2): 551–577.

Chhabra, A. 2005. Beyond Markowitz: A Comprehensive Wealth Allocation Framework for Individual Investors. *Journal of Portfolio Management* 7(5): 8–34.

CNO/FBA. 2015. *Methodology for Computing Short-Term Zero-Coupon Curve as of Euribor Future Rates*. Comité de Normalisation Obligataire/French Bond Association.

Deguest, R., L. Martellini, V. Milhau, A. Suri and H. Wang. 2015. *Introducing a Comprehensive Risk Allocation Framework for Goals-Based Wealth Management*. EDHEC-Risk Institute.

DeMiguel, V., L. Garlappi and R. Uppal. 2009. Optimal versus Naive Diversification: How Inefficient Is the $1/N$ Portfolio Strategy? *Review of Financial Studies* 22(5): 1915–1953.

Duffie, D. 2001a. *Dynamic Asset Pricing Theory*. Princeton University Press. 2001b. *Dynamic Asset Pricing Theory*, 3rd edition. Princeton University Press.

Föllmer, H. and P. Leukert. 1999. Quantile Hedging. *Finance and Stochastics* 3(3): 251–273.

Gürkaynak, R., B. Sack and J. Wright. 2007. The US Treasury Yield Curve: 1961 to the Present. *Journal of Monetary Economics* 54(8): 2291–2304.

Harvey, C. R., Y. Liu and H. Zhu. 2016. ... and the Cross-Section of Expected Returns. *Review of Financial Studies* 29(1): 5–68.

Holzmann, R. and R. Hinz. 2005. *Old Age Income Support in the 21st Century: An International Perspective on Pension Systems and Reform*. Oxford University Press.

Kim, T. and E. Omberg. 1996. Dynamic Nonmyopic Portfolio Behavior. *Review of Financial Studies* 9(1): 141–161.

Kobor, A. and A. Muralidhar. 2018. How a New Bond Can Greatly Improve Retirement Security. Working paper.

Liu, J. 2007. Portfolio Selection in Stochastic Environments. *Review of Financial Studies* 20(1): 1–39.

Maeso, J.-M. and L. Martellini. 2017. Measuring Volatility Pumping Benefits in Equity Markets. Working paper.

Malkiel, B. G. 1996. *A Random Walk Down Wall Street: Including a Life-Cycle Guide to Personal Investing*. W. W. Norton & Company.

Markowitz, H. 1952. Portfolio Selection. *Journal of Finance* 7(1): 77–91.

Martellini, L. and V. Milhau. 2012. Dynamic Allocation Decisions in the Presence of Funding Ratio Constraints. *Journal of Pension Economics and Finance* 11(4): 549–580.

2015. *Factor Investing: A Welfare-Improving New Investment Paradigm or Yet Another Marketing Fad?* EDHEC-Risk Institute.

Martellini, L., P. Priaulet and S. Priaulet. 2003. Deriving the Zero-Coupon Yield Curve. In *Fixed-Income Securities: Valuation, Risk Management and Portfolio Strategies*, chapter 4. John Wiley & Sons, 96–158.

McCulloch, J. H. 1971. Measuring the Term Structure of Interest Rates. *Journal of Business* 44(1): 19–31.

1975. The Tax-Adjusted Yield Curve. *Journal of Finance* 30(3): 811–830.

Merton, R. 1969. Lifetime Portfolio Selection under Uncertainty: The Continuous-Time Case. *Review of Economics and Statistics* 51(3): 247–257.

1971. Optimal Portfolio and Consumption Rules in a Continuous-Time Model. *Journal of Economic Theory* 3(4): 373–413.

1973. An Intertemporal Capital Asset Pricing Model. *Econometrica* 41(5): 867–887.

1974. On the Pricing of Corporate Debt: The Risk Structure of Interest Rates. *Journal of Finance* 29(2): 449–470.

1992. An Intertemporal Capital Asset Pricing Model. In Merton, R., ed., *Continuous-Time Finance*. Blackwell Publishers, 475–523.

Merton, R. and A. Muralidhar. 2017. Time for Retirement "SelFIES"? Working paper.

Modigliani, F. and R. Sutch. 1966. Innovations in Interest Rate Policy. *American Economic Review* 56(2): 178–197.

Moore, K. L. 2011. An Overview of the US Retirement Income Security System and the Principles and Values It Reflects. *Comp. Labor Law & Pol'y Journal* 33(5).

Morningstar. 2018. *2018 Target-Date Fund Landscape*. Morningstar Manager Research.

Muralidhar, A. 2015. *New Bond Would Offer a Better Way to Secure DC Plans*. Pensions and Investments.

Muralidhar, A., K. Ohashi and S. H. Shin. 2016. The Most Basic Missing Instrument in Financial Markets: The Case for Forward Starting Bonds. *Journal of Investment Consulting* 47(2): 34–47.

Nelson, C. R. and A. F. Siegel. 1987. Parsimonious Modeling of Yield Curves. *Journal of Business* 60(4): 473–489.

OECD. 2015. *Pensions at a Glance 2015: OECD and G20 Indicators*.

2016a. *OECD Core Principles of Private Pension Regulation*.

2016b. *Pensions Outlook 2016.*

2017. *Pensions at a Glance 2017: OECD and G20 Indicators.*

Pashchenko, S. 2013. Accounting for Non-Annuitization. *Journal of Public Economics* 98: 53–67.

Samuelson, P. 1969. Lifetime Portfolio Selection by Dynamic Stochastic Programming. *Review of Economics and Statistics* 51(3): 239–246.

Scientific Beta. 2018. Scientific Beta Universe Construction Rules. Scientific Beta. Available at www.scientificbeta.com/#/documentation/ground-rules/eri-scientific-beta-universe-construction-rules.

2019. Scientific Beta Index Calculation Rules. Scientific Beta. Available at www.scientificbeta.com/#/documentation/ground-rules/eri-scientific-beta-strategy-calculation-rules.

Scott, J. S., W. F. Sharpe and J. G. Watson. 2009. The 4% Rule – At What Price? *Journal of Investment Management* 7(3): 31–48.

Svensson, L. E. 1994. *Estimating and Interpreting Forward Interest Rates: Sweden 1992–1994.* National Bureau of Economic Research.

Teplá, L. 2001. Optimal Investment with Minimum Performance Constraints. *Journal of Economic Dynamics and Control* 25(10): 1629–1645.

Thaler, R. H. and S. Benartzi. 2004. Save More Tomorrow™: Using Behavioral Economics to Increase Employee Saving. *Journal of Political Economy* 112(S1): S164–S187.

Vasicek, O. 1977. An Equilibrium Characterization of the Term Structure. *Journal of Financial Economics* 5(2): 177–188.

Vasicek, O. A. and H. G. Fong. 1982. Term Structure Modeling Using Exponential Splines. *Journal of Finance* 37(2): 339–348.

Wachter, J. 2003. Risk Aversion and Allocation to Long-Term Bonds. *Journal of Economic Theory* 112(2): 325–333.

Waggoner, D. 1997. Spline Methods for Extracting Interest Rate Curves from Coupon Bond Prices. Federal Reserve Bank of Atlanta. Working Paper Series, 97–10.

Willis Tower Watson. 2017. Global Pensions Asset Study 2017. Available at www.willistowerswatson.com/-/media/WTW/PDF/Insights/2017/01/global-pensions-asset-study-2017.pdf, retrieved April 10, 2019.

Wooten, J. A. 2001. "The Most Glorious Story of Failure in the Business": The Studebaker-Packard Corporation and the Origins of ERISA. *Buffalo Law Review* 49: 683–739.

Cambridge Elements ☰

Quantitative Finance

Riccardo Rebonato

EDHEC Business School

Editor Riccardo Rebonato is Professor of Finance at EDHEC Business School and holds the PIMCO Research Chair for the EDHEC Risk Institute. He has previously held academic positions at Imperial College, London, and Oxford University and has been Global Head of Fixed Income and FX Analytics at PIMCO, and Head of Research, Risk Management and Derivatives Trading at several major international banks. He has previously been on the Board of Directors for ISDA and GARP, and he is currently on the Board of the Nine Dot Prize. He is the author of several books and articles in finance and risk management, including Bond *Pricing and Yield Curve Modelling* (2017, Cambridge University Press).

About the Series

Cambridge *Elements in Quantitative Finance* aims for broad coverage of all major topics within the field. Written at a level appropriate for advanced undergraduate or graduate students and practitioners, *Elements* combines reports on original research covering an author's personal area of expertise, tutorials and masterclasses on emerging methodologies, and reviews of the most important literature.

Cambridge Elements ☰

Quantitative Finance

Printed in the United States
By Bookmasters